fat-free
BARBECUES

fat-free
BARBECUES

CONSULTANT EDITOR
MADELINE WESTON

HERMES HOUSE

First published in 1999 by Hermes House

HERMES HOUSE books are available for bulk purchase for sales promotion
and for premium use. For details, write or call the sales director,
Hermes House, 27 West 20th Street, New York, NY 10011; (800) 354-9657

© Anness Publishing Limited 1999

Hermes House is an imprint of
Anness Publishing Inc.

ISBN 1 84038 201 5

Publisher: Joanna Lorenz
Project Editor: Zoe Antoniou
Editorial Reader: Richard McGinlay
Production Controller: Mark Fennell
Designer: Ian Sandom
Photographers: Karl Adamson, David Armstrong, Steve Baxter, James Duncan, Michelle Garrett, Amanda
Heywood, David Jordan, Don Last, William Lingwood, Patrick McLeavey, Thomas Odulate and Juliet Piddington
Recipes: Catherine Atkinson, Janet Brinkworth, Kit Chan, Jacqueline Clark, Carole Clements, Patrizia Diemling,
Nicola Diggins, Matthew Drennan, Joanna Farrow, Christine France, Silvana Franco, Sarah Gates, Rosamund Grant,
Janine Hosegood, Shehzad Husain, Christine Ingram, Peter Jordan, Manisha Kanani, Masaki Ko, Gilly Love, Lesley
Mackley, Sue Maggs, Sallie Morris, Annie Nichols, Anne Sheasby, Jenny Stacey, Liz Trigg, Steven Wheeler, Judy
Williams and Elizabeth Wolf-Cohen

For all recipes, quantities are given in both metric and imperial measures and, where appropriate, measures are
also given in standard cups and spoons. Follow one set, but not a mixture,
because they are not interchangeable.

Printed and bound in Hong Kong

1 3 5 7 9 10 8 6 4 2

CONTENTS

INTRODUCTION

The barbecue is one of those special ways of entertaining that appeals to virtually everyone. Food that is cooked over charcoal and eaten alfresco always seems to have twice the flavor of the same dish cooked under the broiler in the kitchen. The tantalizing aroma of grilled chicken, vegetables or fruit whets the appetite in a way that absolutely nothing else can.

However, health concerns have often gone by the wayside when cooking over coals—a lot of people think that food must be liberally doused with oil to keep it moist in the heat of the charcoal. Most of us know that reducing our intake of fat (especially saturated fats) also reduces our risk of heart disease. But up to now, there has been little encouragement for the health-conscious to extend low-fat cooking to the barbecue.

The recipes collected here show how you can cook spicy grills of meat, poultry and fish, flavored with easy marinades—without losing any of the flavor or tenderness. Indeed, the technique of marinating is designed both to flavor and to tenderize—and you will learn how to cut down oil to the bare minimum and, on occasion, to abandon it altogether.

Vegetarian dishes, refreshing salsas, and accompanying salads are all included in this selection, as well as grilled fruit desserts and cooling fruit drinks and ices. All the recipes are so low in fat as to be virtually fat-free, but you will be delighted to find that your barbecues are more delicious than ever.

Choosing a Grill

There is a huge choice of grills on the market, and it's important to choose one that suits your needs. First, decide how many people you usually cook for and where you are likely to use the grill. For instance, do you usually have barbecues just for the family, or are you going to have barbecue parties for lots of friends? Once you've decided on your basic requirements, you will be able to choose among the different types more easily.

Hibachi grills
These small cast-iron grills originated in Japan— *hibachi* translates literally as "firebowl." They are inexpensive, easy to use and transportable. Lightweight versions are now made in steel or aluminum.

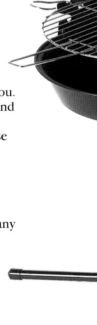

Disposable grills
These will last for about an hour, and are a convenient way of cooking for picnic-style barbecues, for example, or for dealing with low quantities of small pieces of food.

Brazier grills
These open grills are suitable for use on a patio or in the yard. Most have legs or wheels, and it's a good idea to check that the height suits you. The grill area can vary in size, and the box may be round or rectangular. It's useful to choose one that has a shelf attached to the side. Other extras may include an electric, battery-powered or clockwork spit; choose one on which you can adjust the height of the spit. Many have a hood, which comes in handy as a windbreak.

Portable grills
These are usually quite light and fold away easily to fit into a car trunk so that you can take them on picnics. Some are even small enough to fit into a backpack.

Permanent grills

These are a good idea if you often have barbecues at home—they can be built simply and cheaply. Choose a sheltered site that is a little way from the house, but with easy access to the kitchen. Permanent grills can be built with ordinary household bricks, but it's best to line the inside with firebricks, which will withstand the heat better. Use a metal shelf for the fuel and a grid at whatever height you choose. Kits are available containing everything you need to build a grill.

Kettle grills

These have a large, hinged lid that can be used as a windbreak; when closed, the lid lets you use the grill rather like an oven. Even large cuts of meat or whole turkeys can be cooked very successfully, as the heat reflected within the dome helps to brown the meat evenly. The heat is easily controlled by the use of efficient air vents. This type of grill can also be used for home-smoking foods.

Gas grills

The main advantage of these is their convenience—the heat is instant and easily controllable. The disadvantage is that they tend to be quite expensive.

Improvised grills

The most basic grills can be built at no cost at all. A pile of stones topped with chicken wire and fueled with driftwood or kindling makes a very efficient one. Alternatively, find a large tin and punch a few holes in it; fill it with charcoal and place a grid on top.

Types of Fuel

If you have a gas or electric grill, you will not need to buy extra fuel, but most other grills use charcoal or wood. Whatever type of grill you have, choose good-quality fuel, and it's important to always store the fuel in a dry place.

Wood chips or herbs
These are designed to be added to the fire to impart a pleasant aroma to the food. They must be soaked in order to make them last longer. Scatter them straight on the coals during cooking, or place them on a metal tray under the grill rack. Packs of hickory or oak chips are easily available, or you can simply scatter twigs of juniper, rosemary, thyme, sage or fennel over the fire for a similarly striking effect.

Lump charcoal
This is made from hardwood (preferably) or softwood, and comes in lumps of varying size. It is easier to ignite than briquettes, but tends to burn up faster.

Coconut-shell charcoal
This is not widely available, but it makes a good fuel for small grills. It's best used on a fire grate with little holes, as the small pieces tend to fall through the gaps.

Self-igniting charcoal
This is lump charcoal or briquettes, treated with a flammable substance that catches fire very easily. It's important to wait until the ignition agent has burned off before you actually cook food over it, or the smell may taint the food.

Charcoal briquettes
These are useful as they burn for a long time with the minimum of smell and smoke. They can, however, take time to ignite.

Wood
Hardwoods such as oak, apple, olive and cherry are best for grilling, as they burn slowly with a pleasant aroma. Softwoods, however, tend to burn too fast and give off sparks and smoke, so they are unsuitable for most grills. Wood fires need constant attention to make sure that they keep an even and steady heat.

Safety Tips

Grilling is a perfectly safe method of cooking if it's done sensibly—use these simple guidelines as a basic checklist to safeguard against accidents. If you have never organized a barbecue before, keep your first few events as simple as possible, with just one or two types of food. When you have mastered the technique of cooking on a grill, you can start to become more ambitious. Soon you will progress from simple burgers for two or three people to meals for large outdoor parties with all your family and friends.

• Make sure the grill is sited on a firm surface and is stable and level before lighting. Once the grill is lit, make sure that it is not moved.

• Keep the grill sheltered from wind, and keep it well away from trees and shrubs.

• Always follow the manufacturer's instructions for your grill, as there are some kinds of grills that use only one type of fuel.

• Don't try to hurry the fire— some fuels may take some time to build up heat. Never pour flammable liquid onto the grill. This is very dangerous.

• Keep children (and pets) away from the fire, and always make sure that the cooking is supervised by adults.

• Light the grill at least 30 minutes before cooking. Put food on it after the flames have died down to avoid too much burning, which can be harmful.

• Keep all raw foods that are yet to be cooked away from those foods that are already cooked and ready to eat. This is to prevent any possibility of the food becoming cross-contaminated.

• Make sure meats such as burgers, sausages and poultry are thoroughly cooked. Test by piercing the thickest part of the flesh: the juices should run clear and the flesh should not have any trace of pink.

• Wash your hands after handling raw meats and before touching other foods; don't use the same utensils for raw ingredients and cooked food.

• Always position the grid over the glowing, not flaming, coals at a sufficient distance to avoid charring the skin or outside of the poultry. Otherwise the outside may be overcooked, or even burned, before the inside is cooked all the way through.

• In case the fire gets out of control, you should have a bucket of sand and a water spray at the ready, with which to douse the flames. It's always better to be prepared than sorry.

• Keep a first-aid kit handy. If anyone does get burned, hold the burn under cold running water right away.

• Trim any excess fat away from meat. Fat is not only unhealthy— it can also cause dangerous flare-ups if too much of it drips onto the hot fuel.

• Use long-handled grilling tools, such as forks, tongs and brushes, for turning and basting food. Keep some oven gloves handy (preferably the extra-long type) in order to protect your hands from the heat.

Above: Keep all perishable foods cold and covered in a refrigerator or cooler until needed.
Left: Take care that marinades and oils are not spilled on the fire when brushing food.

Grilling Tools and Equipment

Special grilling tools are by no means essential, and you can often use what you already have at home. However, many of them actually make the job easier and often safer. The following are some of the best ones on the market.

Long-handled grilling tools
These should include a pair of tongs, a fork and a flat turner for turning and lifting foods. Choose tools with wood or heatproof handles, so they do not get too hot to hold.

Long-handled basting brushes
These are useful both for basting food and for oiling the grill rack. Choose those with real bristles, rather than nylon, which could melt or burn in use.

Skewers
For kebabs, flat metal skewers are good, particularly with meats, as they conduct the heat well; many have long heat-proof handles or even hand shields. Bamboo and wooden skewers are inexpensive and disposable. They're good for all types of food, but should be soaked in water before use to prevent them from burning.

Hinged wire racks
These are useful for cooking and turning delicate items, such as whole fish, to prevent them from breaking up.

Oven gloves
Thick oven gloves or a cloth will protect your hands from the fire. Make sure that you choose well-padded cloth gloves—not thin ones that will not do the job.

Apron
An apron will protect you and your clothes from the fire and spattering food. It should be made from heavy-duty cotton, rather than plastic-coated.

Meat thermometer
A good thermometer will give a reading of the inside temperature of a large piece of meat. Take care not to touch the bone or the spit when you insert it, or you may get a false reading.

Chopping board
Use a heavy wooden or plastic board for cutting up food. Use different boards for meat to avoid cross-contamination.

Knife
Use a good sharp knife and again, avoid cross-contamination by using a different one for meat.

Water spray
Similar to the type used for spraying houseplants, this is useful for cooling the fire or dousing flames if it gets too hot.

Stiff wire brush
Use this or an abrasive pad and scraper to clean grill racks after cooking. Use with a detergent or a special spray-on cleaner. It is easier to clean the racks if they have been soaked.

oven glove

apron

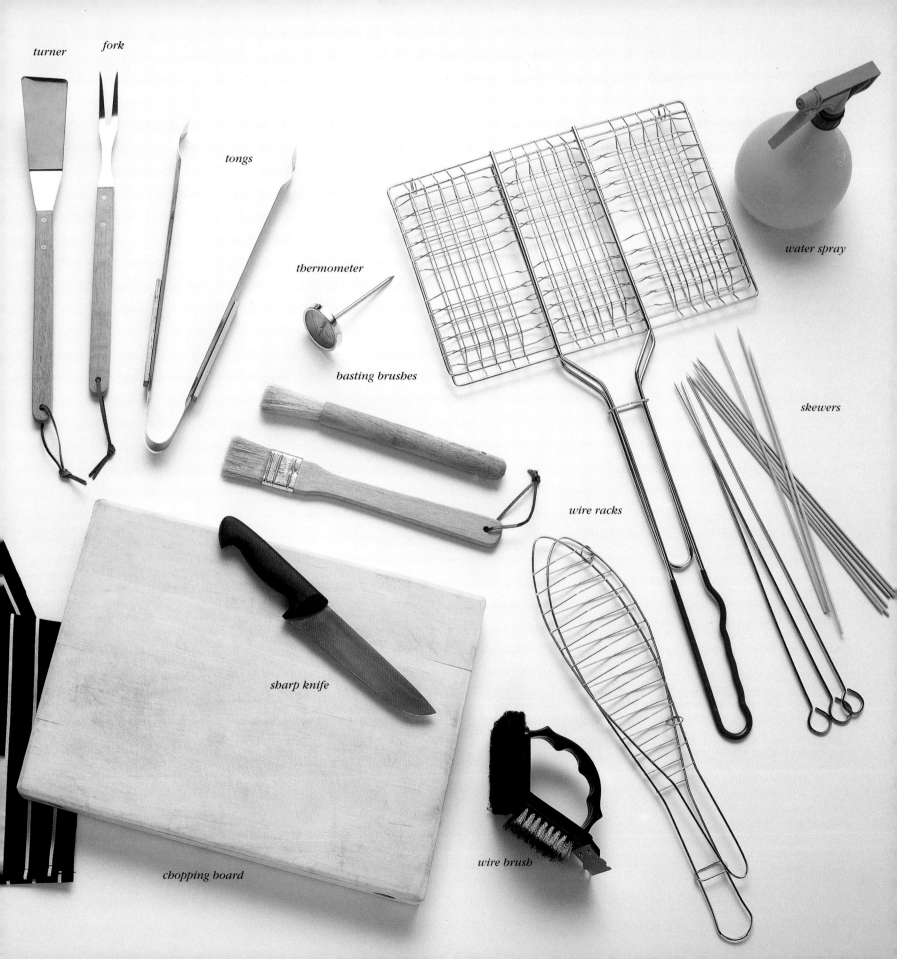

turner

fork

tongs

thermometer

basting brushes

water spray

skewers

wire racks

sharp knife

wire brush

chopping board

Cooking Fat-free Barbecues

Grilling can provide a very healthy and delicious way to cook food. However, it is the types of food that you choose to prepare and the ingredients used in marinating and basting them that will determine whether the fat content of your meal is high or low.

Eating a low-fat diet

A low-fat diet plays an important part in any healthy lifestyle. The amount of fat that we consume is affected by two main factors—the type of foods we eat most often and the way in which we prepare and cook them.

Grilling and broiling are the healthiest ways to cook, particularly because a certain amount of fat within the food will drip away during the cooking process. This method takes you halfway toward eating a low-fat diet. The second factor, the type of foods we eat, also plays a crucial role in determining whether your meal is healthy or not, so make sure you choose your ingredients well.

It is useful to know something about different fats before we can make changes to the way we eat. Some types are more harmful than others, but a little fat is essential for a healthy diet. Knowledge of the different types of fat that exist in food will help you to choose not only what foods you grill but also the ingredients that will be used in your marinades.

It is important, however, that fat is not entirely eliminated from our diets—it is neither possible, nor healthy. Therefore, the definition of "fat-free" for the purpose of this book is a meal containing 5 g or less of fat.

• Saturated fats

These include butter and meat fat, which are solid at room temperature, and are thought to be a major factor in the development of heart disease.

• Monounsaturated fats

These are, in fact, thought to possibly help reduce the blood cholesterol level. They are found in olive oil, rapeseed oil, some nuts, oily fish and avocados.

• Polyunsaturated fats

These fats are found in some soft margarines and sunflower oil, and experts believe they should be eaten in moderation.

Nutritionists recommend that total daily fat consumption should not exceed 30 percent of a person's daily calories. Saturated fat should be 10 percent or less. It is important to cut down on fats, particularly saturated ones.

Choosing food for barbecues

Meat and poultry must be selected carefully. Red meats, such as lamb and beef, are particularly high in saturated fats and must be avoided, or at least kept to a minimum. Chicken and turkey are the ideal meats to cook, either in pieces or on skewers. Try to remove the skin from these meats, as by doing this, you are virtually halving the fat content of your meal.

Fish and shrimp are wonderful when cooked on the grill. Choose white fish such as cod, swordfish or monkfish rather than oily fish such as sardines.

Vegetables can be used to make equally delicious kebabs that are very low in fat. You could place corn on the cob and potatoes wrapped in foil on the grill. Squares of tofu, or bean curd, make a great meat substitute that is very low in fat.

Marinating and basting

Choose your marinade ingredients with care. If you use oil, choose olive oil, but try to replace most of it with other ingredients, such as citrus juices or fat-free yogurts mixed with spices, to create some exciting and varied flavors.

It is important to baste the food with the marinade to keep it moist, but do this sparingly, so you are not replacing oil that has already dripped away. Brush once just before you turn the food during cooking. If the food becomes dry, squeeze on a little citrus juice to keep it moist.

Above: Vegetable and plant oils and some margarines are high in polyunsaturates.
Left: Brush only a little oil onto food before grilling, or replace the oil with a fat-free marinade or citrus juices.

Tips for reducing the fat and not the flavor

It is possible to make the most delicious and exciting yet fat-free barbecues for your family and friends if you keep to some basic rules. There are in fact so many different foods you can cook and so many different ways to flavor them that the end result will always be delectable, if you are imaginative with your ingredients.

• Herbs, spices and crushed garlic can be rubbed into skinless chicken pieces before cooking; if you are cooking in the skin (to remove later), pierce the skin with a knife and insert the flavorings snugly underneath.

• Sprinkle herbs over the coals with herbs, such as rosemary sprigs, to allow a subtle aroma to seep into the meat as it cooks.

• Make marinades of wine, cider, vinegar or lemon or lime juice to provide liquid in place of large amounts of oil. Marinate skinned or slashed chicken pieces in the refrigerator for at least 30 minutes to flavor and tenderize them.

• Sprinkle finely chopped shallots, onions or scallions over poultry pieces for a particularly tangy taste.

• Before cooking, spread chicken breasts with prepared mustard marinades to moisten and add piquant flavor.

• Serve grilled chicken with a salsa or relish, made from a selection of finely chopped fruit or vegetables, scallions and chopped fresh herbs. This will add flavor to pita-bread kebabs.

• Fish only needs a short marinating time—if it is left too long, the acid in the marinade will start to "cook" the flesh. Seafood such as squid, however, can be marinated for up to an hour to tenderize, and only needs very quick cooking over high heat.

• Grill fish in its skin. This helps to keep it moist and easier to skin after cooking.

• When using fromage frais or yogurt in marinades or dips, use reduced fat, low-fat and fat-free versions. Such marinades create a succulent thick coating.

• A marinade made from low-fat yogurt and flavored with Indian pastes, garlic and herbs will adhere to chicken pieces better than a liquid marinade, which tends to drip off. It is also a most effective tenderizer.

• If you want to barbecue larger pieces of poultry, such as a whole bird, make a loose "hood" of foil to reflect the heat back, so that it is cooked from both sides. This also prevents drying and reduces the need for basting.

• Don't forget that how you serve your grilled food will also influence the fat content. Choose salads with light dressings and fat-free dips, together with whole-wheat rolls and pita breads as an accompaniment, for a healthy and substantial meal.

• If you have to use oil, choose olive, corn, sunflower, soy, rapeseed and peanut oils, which are low in saturates. Use the minimum amount for brushing or in marinades, and make up the difference with lemon juice, which is a natural tenderizer.

• Cook small vegetables, potatoes or fish in foil parcels. Add citrus-based marinades to fish and vegetables to add flavor.

Below: Use spices such as (clockwise from top) green cardamom, mixed peppercorns, chiles, ground turmeric, cayenne pepper, caraway seeds and cinnamon sticks.

Fat-free Marinades

The type of marinade you use for grilling affects both the flavor and fat content of your food. Here is a delicious selection of more unusual ideas for you to try that are fat-free.

Keeping the flavor

Marinades are used to add flavor, moisten and tenderize foods, particularly meat, poultry and fish. Marinades usually contain citrus fruit juices or vinegar, but you can add all kinds of ingredients to create any kind of flavor, savory or sweet, hot and spicy or fruity and fragrant. Experiment with more unusual combinations, such as cinnamon and cloves in red wine, or orange juice with cracked peppercorns.

In general, if the fat content of the food is very low, you'll need a little oil in the marinade. Chicken breasts or white fish need some oil, but you can keep this to a minimum by replacing most of the oil with other ingredients, such as fat-free yogurt.

To marinate, combine the ingredients and mix with any poultry or meat. Cover and chill (this is not so important for vegetables). Use the times given in the recipes as your guides—marinating for too long may spoil delicate fish, but too short a time may mean that the flavors have not been absorbed. Tough meat or poultry can be marinated overnight. Use just a little to baste once during cooking, to keep the food moist.

BASIC MARINADE

This can be used for meat or fish.

1 garlic clove, crushed
1 tablespoon sunflower or olive oil
3 tablespoons dry sherry
2 tablespoons Worcestershire sauce
2 tablespoons dark soy sauce
freshly ground black pepper

GINGER AND LIME MARINADE

For meat, poultry or fish.

finely grated rind of 1 lime
juice of 1 lime
1 tablespoon olive oil
1 tablespoon green cardamom pods, seeded and crushed
1-inch piece fresh ginger root, peeled and grated
1 large garlic clove, crushed

HONEY CITRUS MARINADE

This is good with chicken or fish.

finely grated rind and juice of 1 lime, 1 lemon and ½ small orange
1 tablespoon sunflower oil
2 tablespoons honey
1 tablespoon soy sauce
1 teaspoon Dijon mustard
freshly ground black pepper

YOGURT SPICE MARINADE

For meat, poultry or fish.

⅔ cup low-fat plain yogurt
1 small onion, finely chopped
1 garlic clove, crushed
1 teaspoon finely chopped fresh root ginger
1 teaspoon ground coriander
1 teaspoon ground cumin
½ teaspoon ground turmeric

HERB MARINADE

This is good for meat, poultry or fish.

½ cup dry white wine
1 tablespoon olive oil
2 tablespoons lemon juice
2 tablespoons finely chopped fresh herbs, such as parsley, thyme, chives or basil
freshly ground black pepper

RED WINE MARINADE

Good with red meats and game.

⅔ cup dry red wine
1 tablespoon olive oil
1 tablespoon red wine vinegar
2 garlic cloves, crushed
2 dried bay leaves, crumbled
freshly ground black pepper

Basic Timing Guide

It is important, particularly when cooking on the grill, to check that food is properly cooked. The timing chart offers a rough guide to cooking times for different foods, but always test to make sure it is cooked through before serving, if unsure.

Basic timing guide for grilling
Accurate cooking times are difficult to judge because the heat will vary according to the size and type of the grill, the type of fuel and the height of the grill from the fire. Cooking times will also be affected by the thickness of the food and its position on the grill.

Always test the food carefully to make sure it is thoroughly cooked. Chicken should be cooked until the juices are clear and the flesh shows no trace of pink. Fish should be cooked until it is just opaque throughout and no longer. Most foods need

turning only once, but small items such as kebabs may need to be turned more frequently to prevent them from burning.

The easiest way to regulate the heat is to adjust the height of the grill; some grills have air vents that also control the heat. For medium heat, the rack should be about 4 inches from the coals. Raise the rack to obtain lower heat, and lower the rack for very high heat. Take care not to allow your food to char.

Type of Food	Weight or Thickness	Heat	Cooking Time (Total)
Chicken			
whole	3½ lb	spit	1–1¼ hours
quarters, leg or breast		medium	30–35 minutes
boneless breasts		medium	10–15 minutes
drumsticks		medium	25–30 minutes
kebabs		medium	6–10 minutes
Fish			
large, whole	5–10 lb	low/medium	allow 10 minutes per 1-in thickness
small, whole	1¼–2 lb	medium/hot	12–20 minutes
sardines		medium/hot	4–6 minutes
fish steaks or fillets	1 in	medium/hot	6–10 minutes
kebabs	1 in	medium	5–8 minutes
large shrimp, in shell		medium	6–8 minutes
large shrimp, shelled		medium	4–6 minutes
scallops/mussels, in shell		medium	until open
scallops/mussels, shelled		medium	5–8 minutes
half lobster		low/medium	15–20 minutes

Grilling without meat
Cooking meat-free products on the grill can be quicker and safer than meat, as well as equally delicious and low in fat.

Cook kebabs made with vegetables for only a few minutes, remembering that these will need frequent turning and sprinkling with a little extra marinade to prevent them from burning. Kebabs made with tofu or paneer cubes will need only a little longer than this.

Potatoes on skewers will need to cook for longer. If cooked in foil, they will need up to an hour.

TECHNIQUES

Lighting the Fire

Follow these basic instructions when you light your fire, unless you have self-igniting charcoal, in which case you should follow the manufacturer's instructions carefully.

1 Spread a layer of foil over the bottom of the grill, to reflect the heat and to make cleaning easier.

2 It's a good idea to spread a layer of wood, charcoal or briquettes on the fire grate about 2 inches deep. Then you can pile the fuel in a small pyramid on top of this, in the center.

3 Push one or two presoaked briquettes into the center of the pyramid or pour about 3 tablespoons of starter fluid into the fuel and leave for 1 minute. Light with a long match or taper and let burn for 15 minutes. Spread the coals evenly, then leave for 30–45 minutes, until the coals are covered with a film of gray ash, before cooking.

Controlling the Heat

There are three basic ways to control the heat of the grill during cooking.

1 Raise or lower the height of the grill rack. Raise it for slow cooking, or use the bottom level for searing foods.

2 Push the burning coals apart for a lower heat; pile them closer together to increase the heat of the fire.

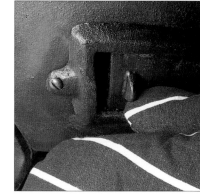

3 Most grills have air vents to allow air to the fire. Open them to make the fire hotter, or close them to lower the temperature.

COOK'S TIP
Try to find an area in the garden or yard with a flat surface where you can set up your grill.

Cooking in Foil Parcels

Delicate foods, or foods that are best cooked slowly in their own steam, can be cooked in foil parcels and either placed directly into the coals of the fire or on the grill rack. You can wrap all kinds of flavorings in the foil parcels too.

1 Use heavy-duty cooking foil and cut two equal pieces to make a double thickness large enough to wrap the food. Lightly brush the center of the foil with a little oil.

2 Place the food in the center of the foil and add any flavorings and seasonings. Pull up the edges of the foil on opposite sides around the food.

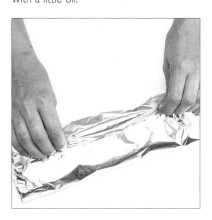

3 Make a double fold in the top of the foil to enclose the food in a parcel.

4 Fold over the ends or twist them together, making sure the parcel is completely sealed, so that the juices cannot escape during cooking.

Preparing Whole Fish for Grilling

Small whole fish are ideal for grilling, especially oily fish such as mackerel or trout. Often they will already be prepared by the fishmonger, but if not they are very simple to prepare at home.

1 Cut off the fins and strip out the gills with scissors.

2 Hold the fish firmly at the tail end and use the back of a small knife blade or a special scaling tool to remove the scales, scraping toward the head end. Rinse under cold water.

3 Cut a long slit under the fish, from just under the tail to just behind the gills, to open up the belly. Use the knife to push out the entrails and discard them. Rinse the fish in cold water.

4 Rub the inside cavity of the fish with salt to clean it properly and rinse again; then dry with absorbent paper towels.

Quick Relish

Making use of pantry ingredients, this relish is ideal for use with kebabs, patties and other quick recipes.

INGREDIENTS
3 tablespoons sweet pickle
1 tablespoon Worcestershire sauce
2 tablespoons ketchup
2 teaspoon prepared mustard
1 tablespoon cider vinegar
2 tablespoons brown sauce

1 Place the sweet pickle in a medium-sized mixing bowl.

2 Stir in the Worcestershire sauce, ketchup and prepared mustard.

3 Add the vinegar and brown sauce and mix well. Chill and use as required.

COOK'S TIP
This is a tangy, tasty relish that is very easy to make.

Tomato Relish

This cooked relish may be served hot or cold. It has a concentrated tomato flavor, making it ideal with pasta, kebabs and barbecued meat.

INGREDIENTS
2 teaspoon olive oil
1 onion, chopped
1 garlic clove, crushed
2 tablespoons flour
2 tablespoons ketchup
1¼ cups passata (sieved tomatoes)
1 teaspoon sugar
1 tablespoon chopped fresh parsley

1 Heat the oil in a pan. Add the onion and garlic clove and sauté for 5 minutes, stirring from time to time.

2 Stir in the flour and cook for another minute.

3 Stir in the ketchup, passata, sugar and fresh parsley. Bring to a boil. Chill and use as required.

COOK'S TIP
Passata is a smooth liquid made from sieved tomatoes. It is used as a base for recipes such as soups and sauces.

Chile Relish

Not for the fainthearted, this warm relish is ideal served with snacks. If you prefer a slightly milder flavor, remove the seeds from the chile before serving. Make sure that you wash your hands thoroughly after handling them.

INGREDIENTS
2 large tomatoes
1 red onion
2 teaspoon chili sauce
1 tablespoon chopped fresh basil
1 green chile, chopped
pinch of salt
pinch of sugar

1 Finely chop the tomatoes and place in a mixing bowl.

2 Finely chop the onion and add to the tomatoes with the chili sauce.

3 Stir in the fresh basil, chile, salt and sugar. Use as required.

COOK'S TIP
Be as generous or as cautious as you like with the chile, depending on how hot you like your food.

Cucumber Relish

A cool, refreshing relish, this may also be used as a dip, or as a sauce to serve with spicy chicken or kebabs. It should be used as quickly as possible—it is at its best when still very fresh, so that the cucumber pieces are still crunchy.

INGREDIENTS
½ cucumber
2 celery stalks, chopped
1 green bell pepper, seeded
    and chopped
1 garlic clove, crushed
1¼ cups low-fat plain yogurt
1 tablespoon chopped fresh cilantro
freshly ground black pepper

1 Dice the cucumber and place in a large bowl.

2 Add the celery, green bell pepper and crushed garlic.

3 Stir in the yogurt and fresh cilantro. Season with the bell pepper. Cover and chill.

COOK'S TIP
All these relishes should be used as quickly as possible, but will keep for up to a week in the refrigerator.

Mango and Radish Salsa

The sweet flavor and juicy texture of mango in this salsa is contrasted very well by the hot and crunchy radishes. Serve with pieces of grilled fish or chicken.

VARIATION
Try using papaya in place of the mango in this salsa.

Serves 4

INGREDIENTS
1 large, ripe mango
12 radishes
juice of 1 lemon
1 tablespoon olive oil
red Tabasco sauce, to taste
3 tablespoons chopped
    fresh cilantro
1 teaspoon pink peppercorns
salt

mango   *radishes*

olive oil

lemon juice

fresh cilantro

red Tabasco sauce

pink peppercorns

NUTRITIONAL NOTES
PER PORTION:

ENERGY 58 Kcals
FAT 2.9 g **SATURATED FAT** 0.5 g
CHOLESTEROL 0
FIBER 2.0 g

1 Holding the mango upright on a cutting board, use a large knife to slice the flesh away from either side of the large flat pit in two pieces. Using a smaller knife, carefully trim away any flesh still clinging to the pit.

2 Score the flesh of the mango halves deeply, taking care to avoid cutting through the skin: make parallel incisions about ½ inch apart; turn and cut lines in the opposite direction. Carefully turn the skin inside out so the flesh stands out. Slice the diced flesh away from the skin.

3 Trim the radishes, discarding the root tails and leaves. Coarsely grate the radishes or dice them finely and place in a bowl with the mango cubes.

4 Stir the lemon juice and olive oil with salt and a few drops of Tabasco sauce to taste, then stir in the chopped fresh cilantro.

5 Coarsely crush the pink peppercorns with a mortar and pestle or place them on a cutting board and flatten them with the heel of a heavy-bladed knife. Stir into the lemon oil.

6 Gently mix together the radishes and mango, then pour in the dressing and toss again. Chill for up to 2 hours before serving.

Fiery Citrus Salsa

This unusual salsa makes a fantastic marinade for fish and is also delicious drizzled over grilled meat.

VARIATION

If you like things really fiery, don't seed the chiles! They will make the salsa particularly hot and fierce.

Serves 4

INGREDIENTS
1 orange
1 green apple
2 fresh red chiles
1 garlic clove
8 fresh mint leaves
juice of 1 lemon
salt and freshly ground black pepper
grilled shrimp, to serve

orange   *apple*

red chiles

garlic

lemon juice

fresh mint

1 Slice the bottom off the orange so that it will stand firmly on a chopping board. Using a sharp knife, remove the peel by slicing from the top to the bottom of the fruit.

2 Hold the orange in one hand over a bowl. Slice toward the middle of the fruit, to one side of a segment, and then gently twist the knife to ease the segment away from the membrane and out of the orange. Repeat to remove all the segments. Squeeze any juice from the remaining membrane into the bowl.

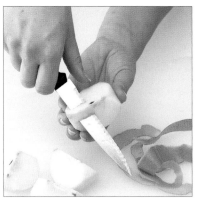

3 Peel the apple, making sure that it is peeled as thinly as possible. Then slice it neatly into wedges and carefully remove the core.

4 Halve the chiles and remove their seeds, then place them in a blender or food processor with the orange segments and juice, apple wedges, garlic and fresh mint.

5 Blend all the contents of the food processor until smooth. Then, with the motor still running, carefully pour in the lemon juice.

6 Season to taste with a little salt and pepper. Pour into a bowl or small jug and serve immediately with grilled shrimp or other kebabs.

NUTRITIONAL NOTES

PER PORTION:

ENERGY 26 Kcals
FAT 0.1 g **SATURATED FAT** 0
CHOLESTEROL 0
FIBER 1.1 g

Chunky Cherry Tomato Salsa

Succulent cherry tomatoes and refreshing cucumber form the basis of this delicious dill-seasoned salsa.

VARIATION
Try flavoring this salsa with other fragrant herbs, such as tarragon, cilantro or even mint.

Serves 4

INGREDIENTS
1 cucumber
1 teaspoon sea salt
1¼ pound cherry tomatoes
1 garlic clove
1 lemon
1 tablespoon chili oil
½ teaspoon dried chili flakes
2 tablespoons chopped fresh dill
salt and freshly ground black pepper

cucumber *cherry tomatoes*

chili flakes *fresh dill*

garlic *chili oil*

sea salt *lemon*

1 Trim the ends off the cucumber and cut it into 1-inch lengths, then cut each piece lengthwise into thin slices.

2 Arrange the cucumber slices in a colander and sprinkle them with the sea salt. Let sit for 5 minutes, until the cucumber has wilted.

3 Wash the cucumber slices well under cold water and pat them dry with paper towels.

4 Quarter the cherry tomatoes and place in a bowl with the wilted cucumber. Finely chop the garlic.

5 Grate the lemon zest finely and place in a small bowl with the juice from the lemon, the chili oil, chili flakes, dill and garlic. Add salt and pepper to taste, and whisk with a fork.

6 Pour the chili oil dressing over the tomato and cucumber and toss well. Let marinate at room temperature for at least 2 hours before serving.

NUTRITIONAL NOTES
PER PORTION:

ENERGY 53 Kcals
FAT 3.3 g **SATURATED FAT** 0.5 g
CHOLESTEROL 0
FIBER 1.6 g

Saffron Dip

Serve this unusual and mild-flavored dip with fresh vegetable crudités—it is particularly good with florets of cauliflower, asparagus tips and baby carrots and corn.

Serves 4

INGREDIENTS
1 tablespoon boiling water
small pinch of saffron strands
scant 1 cup fat-free fromage frais
10 fresh chives
10 fresh basil leaves
salt and freshly ground black pepper
vegetable crudités, to serve

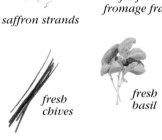

saffron strands

fat-free fromage frais

fresh chives

fresh basil

NUTRITIONAL NOTES
PER PORTION:

ENERGY 30 Kcals
FAT 0.1 g **SATURATED FAT** 0.05 g
CHOLESTEROL 0.5 mg
FIBER 0.05 g

1 Pour the boiling water into a bowl and add the saffron strands. Let infuse for 3 minutes.

2 Beat the fromage frais in a large bowl until smooth. Stir in the infused saffron liquid with a wooden spoon.

3 Snip the chives into the dip. Tear the basil leaves into small pieces and stir them in. Mix thoroughly.

4 Add salt and freshly ground black pepper to taste. Serve the dip with fresh vegetable crudités, if you like.

Potato Skins with Spicy Cajun Dip

As an alternative to deep-frying, grilling potato skins crisps them up in no time and gives them a wonderful charbroiled flavor. This spicy dip makes the perfect partner.

Serves 4

INGREDIENTS
4 large baking potatoes
1 tablespoon olive oil, for brushing
1 cup low-fat plain yogurt
2 garlic cloves, crushed
2 teaspoons tomato paste
1 teaspoon green chili paste or
    1 small green chile, chopped
$\frac{1}{2}$ teaspoon celery salt
salt and freshly ground black pepper

baking potatoes

olive oil

garlic

low-fat yogurt

green chili paste

tomato paste

celery salt

1 Prick the potatoes with a fork, then bake or microwave until tender. Cut them in half and scoop out the flesh, leaving a thin layer of potato on the skins. The scooped out potato can be reserved in the refrigerator or freezer for another meal.

2 Cut each potato shell in half again and lightly brush the skins with olive oil. Cook on a medium-hot grill for 4–5 minutes, or until crisp.

3 Mix together the remaining ingredients in a bowl to make the dip. Serve the potato skins with the Cajun dip on the side.

COOK'S TIP

If you don't have any chili paste or fresh chiles, add one or two drops of hot pepper sauce to the dip instead. Make the dip hot or mild, according to taste.

NUTRITIONAL NOTES
PER PORTION:

ENERGY 293 Kcals
FAT 2.1 g **SATURATED FAT** 0.5 g
CHOLESTEROL 2.5 mg
FIBER 4.9 g

Guacamole with Crudités

This fresh-tasting spicy dip is made using peas instead of the traditional avocados for a light and fat-free version.

Serves 4

INGREDIENTS

2¼ cups frozen peas, defrosted
1 garlic clove, crushed
2 scallions, trimmed
    and chopped
1 teaspoon finely grated zest and juice
    of 1 lime, plus extra juice
    to serve
½ teaspoon ground cumin
dash of Tabasco sauce
1 tablespoon reduced-calorie
    mayonnaise
2 tablespoons chopped fresh cilantro
salt and freshly ground black pepper
pinch of paprika and lime slices,
    to garnish
baby carrots, celery stalks, apples,
    pears and baby corn, to serve

peas   *scallions*

garlic   *ground cumin*

Tabasco sauce   *fresh cilantro*

reduced calorie mayonnaise   *lime*

1 Mix the peas, garlic clove, scallions, lime zest and juice, cumin, Tabasco sauce, mayonnaise and salt and pepper in a food processor or a blender for a few minutes until smooth.

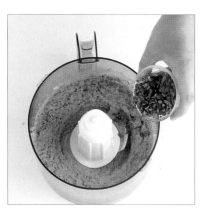

2 Add the chopped cilantro and process for a few more seconds. Spoon into a serving bowl, cover with plastic wrap and chill in the refrigerator for 30 minutes, to let the flavors develop.

3 Prepare the fruit and vegetables for the crudités. Trim and peel the carrots. Halve the celery stalks lengthwise and trim into sticks the same length as the carrots. Quarter, core and thickly slice the apples and pears, then dip into the extra lime juice. Arrange all the prepared crudités with the baby corn on a platter to serve with the guacamole.

4 Sprinkle the paprika over the guacamole and garnish with lime slices.

NUTRITIONAL NOTES
PER PORTION:

ENERGY 112 Kcals
FAT 1.9 g **SATURATED FAT** 0.2 g
CHOLESTEROL 0
FIBER 6.7 g

Tsatziki

You can serve this classic Greek dip with strips of pita bread toasted on the grill. The tangy cucumber makes it a light, refreshing snack.

Serves 4

INGREDIENTS
1 mini cucumber
4 scallions
1 garlic clove
scant 1 cup low-fat plain yogurt
3 tablespoons chopped fresh mint
salt and freshly ground black pepper
fresh mint sprig, to garnish (optional)
toasted pita bread, to serve

mini cucumber   *garlic*

scallions   *low-fat plain yogurt*

fresh mint

1 Trim the ends from the cucumber, then cut it into ¼-inch dice.

2 Trim the scallions and garlic, then chop both very finely.

3 Beat the yogurt until smooth, if necessary, then gently stir in the cucumber, onions, garlic and mint.

4 Transfer the mixture to a serving bowl and add salt and plenty of freshly ground black pepper to taste. Chill until ready to serve and then garnish with a small mint sprig, if liked. Serve with slices of pita bread that have been toasted on the grill, if you like.

NUTRITIONAL NOTES

PER PORTION:

ENERGY 34 Kcals
FAT 0.5 g **SATURATED FAT** 0.25 g
CHOLESTEROL 2 mg
FIBER 0.4 g

COOK'S TIP

Choose low-fat plain yogurt for this dip—it has a delicious creamy texture without the fat of regular plain yogurt. You can find it in most large supermarkets.

Chicken and Pineapple Kebabs

This chicken has a delicate tang and is very tender. The pineapple gives a slight sweetness to the chicken and keeps it succulent during cooking.

NUTRITIONAL NOTES
PER PORTION:
ENERGY 94.8 Kcals
FAT 2.2 g **SATURATED FAT** 0.6 g
CHOLESTEROL 19.8 mg
FIBER 1.2 g

Serves 6

INGREDIENTS
8 ounces can pineapple chunks in natural juice
1 teaspoon ground cumin
1 teaspoon ground coriander
1 small garlic clove, crushed
1 teaspoon chili powder
1 teaspoon salt
2 tablespoons low-fat plain yogurt
1 tablespoon chopped fresh cilantro
few drops of orange food coloring (optional)
10 ounces skinless, boneless chicken breasts
1/2 red bell pepper
1/2 yellow or green bell pepper
1 large onion
9 cherry tomatoes
2 teaspoon corn oil
salad or boiled rice, to serve

chicken breasts

ground cumin

ground coriander

low-fat yogurt

chili powder

garlic

fresh cilantro

pineapple

bell peppers

salt

onion

cherry tomatoes

corn oil

1 Drain the pineapple juice into a bowl. Reserve 12 large chunks of pineapple; squeeze the juice from the remaining chunks into the bowl and set aside. You should have 1/2 cup of pineapple juice. Make up with water if necessary.

2 In a large mixing bowl, combine the ground cumin, ground coriander, garlic, chili powder, salt, yogurt, fresh cilantro and food coloring, if using. Pour in the reserved pineapple juice and mix well.

3 Cut the chicken into bite-size cubes, add to the yogurt and spice mixture, cover and let marinate for 1–1 1/2 hours in a cool place. Meanwhile cut the bell peppers and onion into bite-size chunks.

4 Drain the chicken pieces, reserving the marinade, and thread onto six wooden or metal skewers, alternating with the vegetables, cherry tomatoes and reserved pineapple chunks.

5 Brush the kebabs with the oil, then grill on a medium-hot barbecue, turning and basting the chicken pieces with the marinade regularly, for 15 minutes, or until the chicken is cooked. Serve with salad or plain boiled rice.

Citrus Kebabs

Serve these succulent chicken kebabs on a bed of lettuce leaves, garnished with sprigs of fresh mint and orange and lemon slices.

Serves 4

INGREDIENTS
4 skinless, boneless chicken breasts
fresh mint sprigs, to garnish
orange, lemon or lime slices,
    to garnish

FOR THE MARINADE
finely grated zest and juice of
    $1/2$ orange
finely grated zest and juice of
    $1/2$ lemon or lime
2 teaspoons olive oil
2 tablespoons honey
2 tablespoons chopped fresh mint
$1/4$ teaspoon ground cumin
salt and freshly ground black pepper

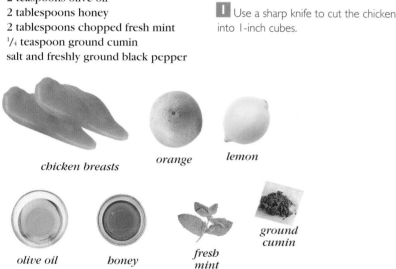

chicken breasts　　*orange*　　*lemon*

olive oil　　*honey*　　*fresh mint*　　*ground cumin*

1 Use a sharp knife to cut the chicken into 1-inch cubes.

NUTRITIONAL NOTES
PER PORTION:

ENERGY 165 Kcals
FAT 5 g **SATURATED FAT** 1.4 g
CHOLESTEROL 53.8 mg
FIBER 0

VARIATION
You can vary the citrus juices if you like—including grapefruit, perhaps, which has a slightly bitter flavor. Garnish the dish with sprigs of fresh cilantro instead of mint.

2 Mix together the marinade ingredients in a large bowl, add the chicken and cover with plastic wrap. Let marinate for at least 2 hours in a cool place, or overnight in the refrigerator.

3 Thread the chicken onto metal skewers and cook on a medium grill for 10 minutes, basting with the marinade and turning frequently. Garnish with mint and citrus slices.

Caribbean Chicken Kebabs

These kebabs have a rich, robust flavor, and the marinade keeps them moist without the need for oil. Serve with a salad or in pita bread pockets.

Serves 4

INGREDIENTS
1¼ pound skinless, boneless chicken breasts
finely grated zest of 1 lime
2 tablespoons fresh lime juice
1 tablespoon rum or sherry
1 tablespoon light brown sugar
1 teaspoon ground cinnamon
2 mangoes, peeled and cubed
rice and salad, to serve

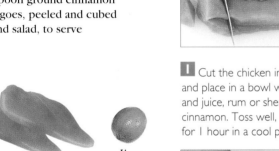

chicken breasts

lime

rum

mangoes

light brown sugar

ground cinnamon

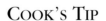

NUTRITIONAL NOTES
PER PORTION:

ENERGY 190 Kcals
FAT 4.1 g **SATURATED FAT** 1.3 g
CHOLESTEROL 53.8 mg
FIBER 1.8 g

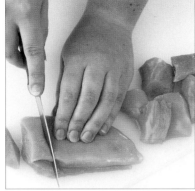

1 Cut the chicken into bite-size chunks and place in a bowl with the lime zest and juice, rum or sherry, sugar and cinnamon. Toss well, cover and let stand for 1 hour in a cool place.

2 Cut the mangoes into cubes by cutting slices, scoring into cubes and slicing away from the skin.

COOK'S TIP
Soak the skewers in cold water for 30 minutes before filling them. This prevents the wood from scorching.

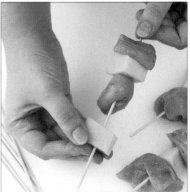

3 Drain the chicken, saving the juices, and thread onto four wooden skewers, alternating with the mango cubes.

4 Grill the skewers on a hot grill for 8–10 minutes, turning occasionally and basting with the juices, until the chicken is tender and golden brown. Serve at once with rice and a salad of your choice, if you like.

Mediterranean Skewers

Grilling intensifies the delicious Mediterranean flavors of the vegetables in this recipe.

Serves 4

INGREDIENTS
2 medium zucchini
1 long thin eggplant
11 ounces boneless turkey, cut into 2-inch cubes
12–16 pearl onions or 4 medium onions, halved
1 red or yellow bell pepper, cut into 2-inch squares

FOR THE MARINADE
3 tablespoons olive oil
3 tablespoons fresh lemon juice
1 garlic clove, finely chopped
2 tablespoons chopped fresh basil
salt and freshly ground black pepper

zucchini

eggplant

turkey

pearl onions

bell pepper

garlic

olive oil

lemon juice

fresh basil

1 Mix the marinade ingredients together in a bowl and set aside.

2 Slice the zucchini and eggplant lengthwise into strips ¼ inch thick. Cut them crosswise about two-thirds down their length. Discard the shorter lengths. Wrap half the turkey with zucchini slices and half with eggplant.

NUTRITIONAL NOTES
PER PORTION:
ENERGY 134 Kcals
FAT 4.6 g **SATURATED FAT** 0.9 g
CHOLESTEROL 45.8 mg
FIBER 1.9 g

3 Prepare the skewers by alternating the turkey, onions and pepper pieces. Sprinkle with the flavored oil. Let marinate for at least 30 minutes.

4 Cook on a medium-hot grill, turning the skewers occasionally, for 10 minutes, or until the turkey is cooked and the vegetables are tender. Serve.

Tandoori Chicken Kebabs

This dish originates from the plains of the Punjab at the foot of the Himalayas, where food is traditionally cooked in clay ovens known as tandoors—hence the name.

Serves 4

INGREDIENTS

4 skinless, boneless chicken breasts
    (about 3½ ounces each)
1 tablespoon lemon juice
3 tablespoons tandoori paste
3 tablespoons low-fat plain yogurt
1 garlic clove, crushed
2 tablespoons chopped fresh cilantro
1 small onion, cut into wedges and
    separated into layers
salt and freshly ground black pepper
fresh cilantro sprigs, to garnish
pilaf rice and naan bread, to serve

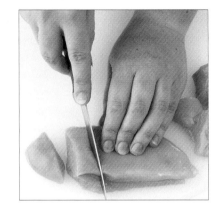
1 Chop the chicken breasts into 1-inch cubes and place in a bowl.

lemon juice *tandoori paste*

chicken breasts

fresh cilantro
onion   *garlic*   *low-fat yogurt*

COOK'S TIP

Use strips of skinless, boneless turkey breasts for a cheaper and equally low-fat alternative. Remember to serve with a fat-free salad for a particularly healthy meal.

NUTRITIONAL NOTES
PER PORTION:

ENERGY 166 Kcals
FAT 5 g **SATURATED FAT** 1.4 g
CHOLESTEROL 56.3 mg
FIBER 0

2 Add the lemon juice, tandoori paste, yogurt, garlic, cilantro and seasoning. Cover and let marinate in the refrigerator for 2–3 hours.

3 Thread alternate pieces of chicken and onion onto four skewers. Cook them over a hot grill for about 10–12 minutes, turning once. Make sure that the onions do not burn. Garnish with cilantro sprigs and serve at once with pilaf rice and naan bread, if liked.

Sweet-and-Sour Kebabs

This marinade contains sugar and will burn very easily, so cook the kebabs slowly and turn them often. Serve with a fat-free salad of your choice.

Serves 4

INGREDIENTS
2 skinless, boneless chicken breasts
8 pearl onions or 2
    medium onions
3 firm bananas
4 lean bacon strips
1 red bell pepper, diced
sprigs of fresh parley to garnish
rice or salad, to serve

FOR THE MARINADE
2 tablespoons brown sugar
1 tablespoon Worcestershire sauce
2 tablespoons lemon juice
salt and freshly ground black pepper

chicken breasts

pearl onions

red bell pepper

bananas

brown sugar

Worcestershire sauce

bacon

lemon juice

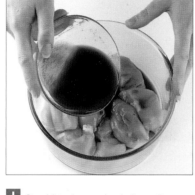

1 Combine the marinade ingredients. Cut each chicken breast into four pieces, add the marinade, cover and let sit for at least 4 hours in the refrigerator.

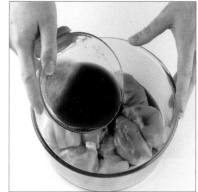

2 Peel the onions, blanch them in boiling water for 5 minutes and drain. Quarter them if using medium onions.

NUTRITIONAL NOTES
PER PORTION:

ENERGY 304 Kcals
FAT 5 g **SATURATED FAT** 1.6 g
CHOLESTEROL 30.5 mg
FIBER 3.4 g

3 Peel all the bananas and cut each one into three or four pieces, depending on the size of the bananas, to make nine or 12 pieces in all. Cut the bacon strips into the same number of pieces and wrap one piece around each banana slice.

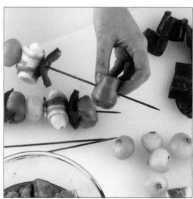

4 Thread the bananas onto skewers with the chicken pieces, onions and pepper pieces. Brush generously with the marinade. Cook on a low grill for 15 minutes, turning frequently and basting when necessary. Serve with rice or salad, and garnish with parsley sprigs.

Turkey Sosaties with a Curried Apricot Sauce

This is a South African way of cooking meat or poultry in a delicious sweet and sour sauce spiced with curry powder.

Serves 4

INGREDIENTS
1 teaspoon vegetable oil
1 onion, finely chopped
1 garlic clove, crushed
2 bay leaves
juice of 1 lemon
2 tablespoons curry powder
4 tablespoons apricot jam
4 tablespoons apple juice
1½ pounds turkey fillet
2 tablespoons low-fat crème fraîche
salt

onion

garlic

bay leaves

apple juice

lemon juice

curry powder

turkey

vegetable oil

apricot jam

low-fat crème fraîche

1 Heat the oil in a saucepan. Add the onion, garlic and bay leaves and cook over low heat for 10 minutes, until the onions are soft. Add the lemon juice, curry powder, apricot jam and apple juice, with salt to taste. Cook gently for 5 minutes. Let cool.

2 Cut the turkey into evenly sized cubes about ¾ inch thick.

3 Add to the apricot marinade. Mix well, cover and let sit in a cool place to marinate for at least 2 hours or overnight in the refrigerator. Thread the turkey onto skewers, allowing the marinade to run back into the bowl. Grill the sosaties over a medium-hot grill for 6–8 minutes, turning several times, until cooked.

4 Meanwhile, transfer the reserved apricot marinade to a pan and simmer gently over low heat for about 2 minutes. Then stir in the crème fraîche and serve immediately with the hot turkey sosaties.

NUTRITIONAL NOTES
PER PORTION:

ENERGY 200 Kcals
FAT 2.8 g **SATURATED FAT** 0.7 g
CHOLESTEROL 83 mg
FIBER 0.8 g

Chicken Pitas with Red Coleslaw

Pitas are convenient for simple snacks and picnics and it's easy to pack in plenty of fresh, healthy ingredients. This recipe is ideal for pieces of chicken breast that have already been grilled.

Serves 4

INGREDIENTS
¼ red cabbage
1 small red onion, finely sliced
2 radishes, thinly sliced
1 red apple, peeled, cored and grated
1 tablespoon lemon juice
3 tablespoons fat-free fromage frais
1 cooked skinless, boneless chicken
    breast, about 6 ounces
4 large or 8 small pita breads
salt and freshly ground black pepper
chopped fresh parsley, to garnish

red cabbage

red onion

red apple

lemon juice

fat-free fromage frais

radishes

pita breads

chicken breast

NUTRITIONAL NOTES
PER PORTION:

ENERGY 293 Kcals
FAT 2.8 g **SATURATED FAT** 0.5 g
CHOLESTEROL 24.5 mg
FIBER 5.5 g

1 Remove the tough central stalk from the cabbage, then finely shred the leaves using a large sharp knife. Place the shredded cabbage in a bowl. Stir in the onion, radishes, apple and lemon juice.

COOK'S TIP
Use freshly cooked pieces of chicken, straight from the grill, removing any bones. You can also use any cold leftover pieces from a barbecue party the day before, as long as the pieces have been refrigerated.

2 Stir the fromage frais into the cabbage mixture and season well. Finely slice the cooked chicken breast and stir into the cabbage mixture until well coated in fromage frais.

3 Toast the pitas on a grill over low heat, then split them along one edge using a round-bladed knife. Spoon the filling into the pitas, then garnish with the chopped fresh parsley.

Bacon Koftas

These koftas are easy to make and are good served with rice and lots of salad. Although bacon can be high in fat in itself, it is used more as a flavoring in this recipe—a very effective way of livening up low-fat food.

Serves 4

INGREDIENTS
6 ounces lean bacon
1 cup fresh whole-wheat
    bread crumbs
2 scallions, chopped
1 tablespoon chopped fresh parsley
finely grated zest of 1 lemon
1 egg white
freshly ground black pepper
paprika, for sprinkling
lemon zest and fresh parsley leaves,
    to garnish
rice and salad, to serve

fresh parsley   *scallions*

lemon   *egg white*   *bacon*

bread crumbs   *paprika*

1 Remove any pieces of fat that may be on the bacon slices and cut them coarsely. Place the bacon in a food processor together with the bread crumbs, scallions, parsley, lemon zest, egg white and pepper. Process the mixture until it is finely chopped and begins to bind together.

VARIATION

You can add virtually anything you like to give flavor to these simple koftas. Use chopped fresh mint or basil instead of the parsley, and a lime instead of the lemon.

2 Divide the bacon mixture into eight pieces and mold into long oval shapes, wrapped around eight wooden or bamboo skewers.

3 Sprinkle the koftas with paprika and cook on a hot grill for 8–10 minutes, turning occasionally, until browned and cooked through. Garnish with lemon zest and parsley leaves, then serve hot with rice and a salad.

COOK'S TIP

Remember to soak the wooden or bamboo skewers before wrapping the bacon koftas around them. This should prevent them from burning on the grill.

Chicken with Lime

Limes can be used in the same way as lemons but provide more of a color contrast—particularly when mixed with fresh cilantro.

Serves 4

INGREDIENTS
4 skinless, boneless chicken breasts
2 limes and 4-6 cilantro sprigs,
    to garnish

FOR THE MARINADE
1 small onion, finely chopped
1 tablespoon finely grated or crushed
    fresh ginger root
1 tablespoon crushed garlic
2 tablespoons dark soy sauce
2 teaspoon ground coriander
1 teaspoon ground cumin
1 tablespoon dark brown sugar
1 tablespoon sunflower oil

chicken breasts

ginger root

dark brown sugar

onion

ground coriander

sunflower oil

garlic

ground cumin

soy sauce

1 Cut the chicken breasts into strips and mix with the marinade ingredients. Cover and set aside in the refrigerator for 4 hours.

2 Using a channel knife, cut decorative strips lengthwise down the skin of one of the limes at ½ inch intervals, then cut the lime into slices about ¼ inch thick. Make a cut from the center of each slice to the edge and twist to an "S" shape. Cut the remaining lime in half lengthwise and place cut side down. Make three V-shaped cuts into each of the lime halves, one below the other, and push each wedge out slightly to give a stepped effect.

3 Drain the chicken strips, reserving the marinade for later use. Thread onto wooden skewers.

4 Cook on a grill over moderately hot coals for about 15 minutes, or until tender, turning frequently and brushing occasionally with the reserved marinade to keep the meat moist. Serve garnished with the limes and cilantro sprigs.

PER PORTION:

ENERGY 161 Kcals
FAT 4.8 g **SATURATED FAT** 1.3 g
CHOLESTEROL 53.7 mg
FIBER 0.2 g

Chicken Tikka

The red food coloring gives this dish its traditional bright color. Serve with lemon wedges and a crisp mixed salad.

Serves 4

INGREDIENTS
4 skinless chicken breasts
lemon wedges and mixed salad
   greens, such as frisée and oak-leaf
   lettuce or radicchio, to serve

FOR THE MARINADE
²/₃ cup low-fat plain yogurt
1 teaspoon paprika
2 teaspoons grated fresh ginger root
1 garlic clove, crushed
2 teaspoons garam masala
¹/₂ teaspoon salt
few drops of red food
   coloring (optional)
juice of 1 lemon

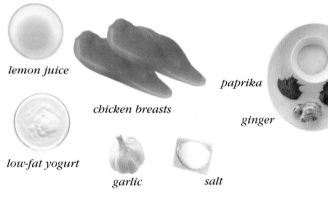

lemon juice

chicken breasts

paprika

ginger

garam masala

low-fat yogurt

garlic

salt

1 Mix all the marinade ingredients in a large dish. Add the chicken pieces to coat for at least 4 hours or overnight in the refrigerator, to allow the flavors to penetrate the flesh.

COOK'S TIP

This is an example of a dish that is usually very high in fat, but with a few basic changes this level can be dramatically reduced. This can also be achieved in other similar dishes, by substituting low-fat yogurt for full-fat versions and creams, by removing skin from chicken, as well as by reducing the amount of oil.

NUTRITIONAL NOTES
PER PORTION:

ENERGY 160 Kcals
FAT 4.3 g **SATURATED FAT** 1.4 g
CHOLESTEROL 54.5 mg
FIBER 0.4 g

2 Remove the chicken pieces from the marinade and cook over a hot grill for 30–40 minutes, or until tender, turning occasionally and basting with a little of the marinade.

3 Arrange on a bed of salad greens with two lemon wedges and serve either hot or cold.

Chicken in Spicy Yogurt

Plan this dish well in advance, as the chicken needs
to marinate for a while to develop a spicy flavor.

NUTRITIONAL NOTES

PER PORTION:

ENERGY 126 Kcals
FAT 3.2 g **SATURATED FAT** 1 g
CHOLESTEROL 43 mg
FIBER 0.1 g

Serves 6

INGREDIENTS
6 chicken pieces
juice of 1 lemon
1 teaspoon salt
lemon or lime wedges and lettuce
    leaves, to garnish

FOR THE MARINADE
1 teaspoon coriander seeds
2 teaspoon cumin seeds
6 cloves
2 bay leaves
1 onion, quartered
2 garlic cloves
2-inch piece fresh ginger root, peeled
    and roughly chopped
½ teaspoon chili powder
1 teaspoon turmeric
⅔ cup low-fat plain yogurt

1 Skin the chicken pieces and make
deep slashes in the fleshiest parts with a
sharp knife. Sprinkle with the lemon
juice and salt and rub in.

2 Spread the coriander and cumin
seeds, cloves and bay leaves in the
bottom of a large frying pan and dry-fry
over moderate heat until the bay leaves
are crispy.

3 Cool the spices and grind coarsely
with a mortar and pestle.

chicken pieces

lemon juice

low-fat yogurt

ginger root

salt

onion

coriander seeds

garlic

cloves

bay leaves

cumin seeds

chili powder

turmeric

4 Finely mince the onion, garlic and
ginger in a food processor or blender.
Add the ground spices, chili powder,
turmeric and yogurt, then strain in the
lemon juice from the chicken.

5 Arrange the chicken in a single layer
in a shallow dish. Pour the marinad over,
then cover and chill for 24–36 hours,
occasionally turning the chicken pieces in
the marinade.

6 Remove the chicken pieces and
cook over a low grill for about 30–45
minutes, turning the pieces and basting
with the marinade occasionally. Serve
hot or cold, garnished with fresh leaves
and wedges of lemon or lime.

Grilled Fish in Banana Leaves

Fish prepared in this way is particularly succulent and flavorful, as well as being easy to grill. Fillets are used here rather than whole fish, which makes it easier for those who don't like to fuss with bones.

Serves 4

INGREDIENTS

6 ounces mixed vegetables, such as
    carrots or leeks
1 cup coconut milk
2 tablespoons red curry paste
3 tablespoons fish sauce
2 tablespoons sugar
5 kaffir lime leaves, torn
4 x 6-ounce fish fillets, such
    as snapper
4 banana leaves or pieces of foil
2 tablespoons shredded scallions,
    to garnish
2 red chiles, finely sliced, to garnish

coconut milk

red curry paste

fish sauce

sugar

lime leaves

fish fillets

banana leaves

mixed vegetables

1 Prepare the vegetables. Wash and peel them as necessary and shred finely. Meanwhile, combine the coconut milk, curry paste, fish sauce, sugar and kaffir lime leaves in a dish. Marinate the fish in the mixture for 15–30 minutes.

2 Mix together the vegetables and lay a portion on top of a banana leaf or piece of foil. Place a piece of fish on top with a little of its marinade.

3 Wrap up the fish in a leaf parcel and secure with toothpicks. (With foil, just crumple the edges together.) Repeat with the rest of the fish.

4 Cook on a medium-hot grill for 20–25 minutes, or until the fish is cooked. Just before serving, garnish the fish with a sprinkling of scallions and sliced red chiles.

NUTRITIONAL NOTES

PER PORTION:

ENERGY 289 Kcals
FAT 4.4 g **SATURATED FAT** 0.9 g
CHOLESTEROL 147 mg
FIBER 1.2 g

Tuna and Corn Fish Cakes

These little tuna fish cakes are quick both to make and to cook on the grill. Use fresh mashed potatoes, or instant, if short on time.

Serves 4

INGREDIENTS
1½ cups cooked, mashed potatoes
7-ounce can tuna in brine, drained
¾ cup canned or frozen corn
2 tablespoons chopped fresh parsley
1 cup fresh white or whole-wheat
    bread crumbs
salt and freshly ground black pepper
lemon wedges and fresh vegetables,
    to serve (optional)

mashed potatoes

tuna

fresh parsley

corn

bread crumbs

1 Place the mashed potato in a bowl and stir in the tuna, corn and chopped parsley.

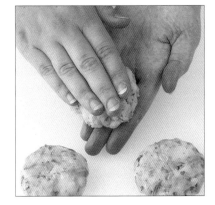

2 Season to taste with salt and pepper, then shape into eight fish cakes with your hands.

NUTRITIONAL NOTES

PER PORTION:

ENERGY 387 Kcals
FAT 2.7 g **SATURATED FAT** 0.2 g
CHOLESTEROL 25 mg
FIBER 2.2 g

VARIATION

For simple variations that are just as good, try using canned sardines, red or pink salmon or smoked mackerel in place of the tuna.

3 Spread out the bread crumbs on a plate and press the fish cakes into the crumbs to coat lightly.

4 Cook the fish cakes over a moderately hot grill until crisp and golden brown, turning once. Take care that they do not break up. Serve immediately with lemon wedges and fresh vegetables, if desired.

Halibut with Fresh Tomato and Basil Salsa

Try using a fish rack for this dish, as halibut breaks easily when the skin has been removed.

Serves 4

INGREDIENTS
4 halibut fillets, about
    5 ounces each
2 teaspoons olive oil

FOR THE SALSA
1 medium tomato, roughly chopped
1/4 red onion, finely chopped
1 small jalapeño pepper
2 tablespoons balsamic vinegar
10 large fresh basil leaves
1 teaspoon olive oil
salt and freshly ground black pepper

halibut fillets

tomato

jalapeño pepper

balsamic vinegar

red onion

olive oil

basil leaves

NUTRITIONAL NOTES
PER PORTION:

ENERGY 202 Kcals
FAT 5 g SATURATED FAT 0.9 g
CHOLESTEROL 61.5 mg
FIBER 0.25 g

1 To make the salsa, mix together the chopped tomato, red onion, jalapeño pepper and balsamic vinegar in a bowl.

2 Slice the fresh basil leaves finely, using a sharp kitchen knife.

VARIATION
Use any other white fish that you can get, such as cod, sole or whiting—it will be just as good.

3 Stir the basil and the olive oil into the tomato mixture. Season to taste. Cover the bowl with plastic wrap and marinate for at least 3 hours.

4 Brush the halibut fillets with oil and season. Cook on a medium grill for 8 minutes, turning once. Serve with the salsa.

Swordfish Kebabs

Swordfish has a firm, meaty texture that makes it ideal for cooking on a grill. Marinate the fish first to keep it moist.

Serves 6

INGREDIENTS
1½ pounds swordfish steaks
1 tablespoon olive oil
juice of 1 lemon
1 garlic clove, crushed
1 teaspoon paprika
2 onions
3 tomatoes
salt and freshly ground black pepper
salad and pita bread, to serve

swordfish steaks

olive oil

garlic

lemon juice

tomatoes

paprika

onions

NUTRITIONAL NOTES
PER PORTION:

ENERGY 137 Kcals
FAT 5 g **SATURATED FAT** 1.1 g
CHOLESTEROL 44 mg
FIBER 0.7 g

1 Use a large kitchen knife to cut the swordfish steaks into large cubes. Arrange the cubes in a single layer in a large shallow dish. Blend together the olive oil, lemon juice, garlic, paprika and seasoning in a bowl, and pour this over the fish. Cover the dish loosely with plastic wrap and marinate in a cool place for up to 2 hours.

2 Peel the onions and cut them into large wedges.

3 Cut each tomato in half and then cut again into quarters.

4 Thread the fish cubes onto metal skewers, alternating them with the pieces of tomato and onion wedges. Cook the kebabs on a hot grill for 5–10 minutes, basting frequently with the remaining marinade and turning occasionally. Serve with salad and warm pita bread.

Grilled Snapper with Hot Mango Salsa

A ripe mango provides the basis for a deliciously rich, fruity salsa. The dressing needs no oil and features the tropical flavors of cilantro, ginger and chile.

Serves 4

INGREDIENTS

4 red snapper, about 9 ounces each, cleaned, scaled and gutted
2 teaspoons olive oil
salt and freshly ground black pepper
lettuce leaves, mixed vegetables, cherry tomatoes and hard-boiled eggs, to serve (optional)

FOR THE SALSA

3 tablespoons chopped fresh cilantro
1 medium ripe mango, peeled, pited and diced
$\frac{1}{2}$ red chile, seeded and chopped
1-inch fresh ginger root, grated
juice of 2 limes
generous pinch of celery salt

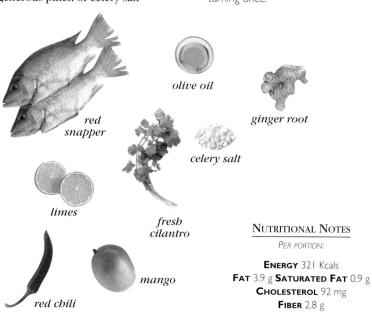

red snapper

limes

olive oil

ginger root

celery salt

fresh cilantro

mango

red chili

1 Using a sharp knife, slash each snapper three times on either side. Brush with the olive oil and cook on a medium-hot grill for 12 minutes, turning once.

2 To make the salsa, place the chopped fresh cilantro in a food processor. Add the mango chunks, chile, grated ginger, lime juice and celery salt and process until smooth.

3 Distribute the lettuce leaves evenly among four large plates.

4 Arrange the snapper on the lettuce and season to taste. Serve immediately with mixed vegetables, cherry tomatoes and hard-boiled eggs, if desired, or substitute a fat-free salad. Accompany the meal with the salsa.

VARIATION

If fresh mangoes are unavailable, use canned ones, draining well. Sea bream can also be used for this recipe, if you prefer.

NUTRITIONAL NOTES
PER PORTION:

ENERGY 321 Kcals
FAT 3.9 g **SATURATED FAT** 0.9 g
CHOLESTEROL 92 mg
FIBER 2.8 g

Calamari with Two-tomato Stuffing

Calamari, or baby squid, are quick to cook, but make sure that you turn and baste them often. Don't overcook them, or they will toughen.

Serves 4

INGREDIENTS

1¼ pounds baby squid, cleaned
1 garlic clove, crushed
3 plum tomatoes, skinned
    and chopped
8 sun-dried tomatoes, chopped
4 tablespoons chopped fresh basil,
    plus extra, to serve
4 tablespoons fresh white
    bread crumbs
1 tablespoon olive oil, plus extra
    for brushing
1 tablespoon red wine vinegar
salt and freshly ground black pepper
lemon wedges and juice, to serve

baby squid

garlic

plum tomatoes

sun-dried tomatoes

bread crumbs

olive oil

red wine vinegar

fresh basil

1 Remove the tentacles from the squid and roughly chop them; leave the main part of the squid whole.

2 Mix together the garlic, plum tomatoes, sun-dried tomatoes, basil and bread crumbs, and stir well. Then stir in the olive oil and the red wine vinegar. Season well with plenty of salt and pepper. Soak some wooden toothpicks in water for at least 10 minutes before use, to prevent them from burning.

3 With a teaspoon, fill the squid with the stuffing mixture. Secure the open ends with the toothpicks.

4 Brush the squid with a little olive oil and cook over a medium-hot grill for 4–5 minutes, turning often. Sprinkle with lemon juice and extra basil to serve, with lemon wedges on the side.

COOK'S TIP

You can often buy ready-prepared squid in packages from good supermarkets, which will save you a lot of time.

NUTRITIONAL NOTES
PER PORTION:

ENERGY 183 Kcals
FAT 4.6 g **SATURATED FAT** 0.8 g
CHOLESTEROL 281 mg
FIBER 0.7 g

Cajun-style Cod

This recipe works equally well with any firm-fleshed fish such as swordfish, shark, tuna or halibut. The herbs and spices here create a wonderful, pungent aroma and a taste that will make your mouth water.

Serves 4

INGREDIENTS

4 cod steaks, each weighing about
   6 ounces
2 tablespoons low-fat plain yogurt
1 tablespoon lime or lemon juice
1 garlic clove, crushed
1 teaspoon ground cumin
1 teaspoon paprika
1 teaspoon mustard powder
½ teaspoon cayenne pepper
½ teaspoon dried thyme
½ teaspoon dried oregano
new potatoes and a mixed salad,
   to serve (optional)

low-fat yogurt

garlic

ground cumin

cayenne pepper

lime

cod

dried thyme

mustard powder

paprika

dried oregano

1 Pat the fish dry with absorbent paper towels. Combine the yogurt and lime or lemon juice and brush lightly over both sides of the fish.

2 Combine the crushed garlic, spices and herbs. Coat both sides of the fish with the seasoning mix, making sure that it is well rubbed in.

3 Cook the fish over a hot grill for 4 minutes, or until the underside is well browned.

4 Turn over and cook for another 4 minutes, or until the steaks have cooked through. Serve immediately, with new potatoes and a mixed salad, if liked.

NUTRITIONAL NOTES

PER PORTION:

ENERGY 172 Kcals
FAT 2.2 g **SATURATED FAT** 0.5 g
CHOLESTEROL 98 mg
FIBER 0

COOK'S TIP

Using a fish rack, or placing a smaller grill pan rack on your barbecue grid, will make it easier to cook fish without it breaking up.

Spiced Shrimp with Vegetables

This is a light and nutritious Indian dish, excellent served either on a bed of lettuce or with rice.

Serves 4

INGREDIENTS
20 cooked jumbo shrimp, peeled
1 medium zucchini, thickly sliced
1 medium onion, cut into 8 chunks
8 cherry tomatoes
8 ears baby corn
mixed salad leaves, to serve

FOR THE MARINADE
2 tablespoons chopped
    fresh cilantro
1 teaspoon salt
2 fresh green chiles, seeded
    if wished
3 tablespoons lemon juice
2 teaspoon olive oil

zucchini

cooked jumbo shrimp

cherry tomatoes

onion

fresh cilantro

baby corn

green chiles

salt

lemon juice

olive oil

1 To make the marinade, blend the cilantro, salt, chiles, lemon juice and oil together in a food processor.

2 Empty the contents from the processor into a bowl.

NUTRITIONAL NOTES
PER PORTION:

ENERGY 95 Kcals
FAT 0.9 g **SATURATED FAT** 0.2 g
CHOLESTEROL 156 mg
FIBER 0.9 g

3 Add the peeled shrimp to the mixture in the bowl and stir to make sure that all the shrimp are well coated. Cover the bowl with plastic wrap and set aside in a cool place to marinate for about 30 minutes.

4 Arrange the vegetables and shrimp alternately on four long skewers. Cook on a medium grill for 5 minutes, turning frequently, until cooked and browned. Serve immediately, on a bed of mixed salad greens.

Monkfish with Peppered Citrus Marinade

Monkfish is a firm, meaty fish that cooks well on the grill and keeps its shape. Serve with a green salad.

NUTRITIONAL NOTES
Per portion:

ENERGY 136 Kcals
FAT 3.8 g **SATURATED FAT** 0.6 g
CHOLESTEROL 22 mg
FIBER 0

Serves 4

INGREDIENTS
2 monkfish tails, about
    11 ounces each
1 lime
1 lemon
2 oranges
handful of fresh thyme sprigs
2 tablespoons olive oil
1 tablespoon mixed peppercorns,
    roughly crushed
salt and freshly ground black pepper

monkfish tails

lime

oranges

lemon

mixed peppercorns

fresh thyme

olive oil

1 Remove any skin from the monkfish tails. Cut carefully down one side of the backbone, sliding the knife between the bone and flesh, to remove the fillet on one side.

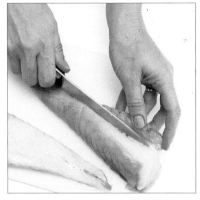

2 Turn the fish and repeat on the other side, to remove the second fillet. Repeat on the second tail. (You could ask your fishmonger to do this for you.) Lay the four fillets out flat.

3 Cut two slices from each of the citrus fruits and arrange them over two of the fillets. Add a few sprigs of thyme and sprinkle with salt and pepper. Finely grate the zest from the remaining fruit and sprinkle it over the fish.

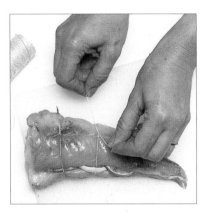

4 Lay the other two fillets on top and tie them firmly at intervals, with fine cotton string, to hold them in shape. Place in a wide dish.

5 Squeeze the juice from the remaining fruits. Mix with the oil and more salt and pepper. Spoon over the fish. Cover and let marinate for 1 hour in a cool place, turning a few times and spooning the marinade over it.

6 Drain the monkfish, reserving the marinade, and sprinkle with the crushed peppercorns. Cook on a medium-hot grill for 15–20 minutes, basting with the marinade and turning occasionally, until evenly cooked.

Marrakesh Monkfish with Chermoula

Chermoula is a Moroccan spice mixture that is used as a marinade for meat, poultry and fish.

Serves 4

INGREDIENTS

1 small red onion, finely chopped
2 garlic cloves, crushed
1 fresh red chile, seeded and
  finely chopped
2 tablespoons chopped fresh cilantro
1 tablespoon chopped fresh mint
1 teaspoon ground cumin
1 teaspoon paprika
generous pinch of saffron strands
4 tablespoons olive oil
juice of 1 lemon
1½ pound monkfish fillets, skinned
salt
salad and pita bread, to serve

red onion   garlic

red chile

fresh cilantro

fresh mint

ground cumin

paprika

saffron

olive oil

lemon juice

monkfish

1 To make the chermoula, mix the onion, garlic, chile, cilantro, mint, cumin, paprika, saffron, olive oil, lemon juice and salt together in a mixing bowl. Set aside.

2 Cut the monkfish into cubes. Add them to the spice mixture in the bowl. Mix well to coat, cover and let sit in a cool place for 1 hour.

3 Thread the monkfish onto skewers and place on the rack over a medium-hot grill. Spoon on a little of the marinade. Grill the monkfish skewers for about 3 minutes on each side, until cooked through and lightly browned. Serve with salad and warm pita bread.

COOK'S TIP

If you use bamboo or wooden skewers, soak them in cold water for about 30 minutes before draining and threading them. This will help to prevent the skewers from scorching.

NUTRITIONAL NOTES

PER PORTION:

ENERGY 139 Kcals
FAT 3.2 g **SATURATED FAT** 0.5 g
CHOLESTEROL 24 mg
FIBER 0.21 g

Jumbo Shrimp with Salsa Verde and Lime

Limes are wonderfully versatile and look great simply cut into pieces, then sprinkled with a little finely chopped cilantro or parsley.

Serves 4

INGREDIENTS
½ cup white wine
2 teaspoons grated fresh ginger root
2 teaspoons crushed garlic
24 raw jumbo shrimp, peeled, with
    heads left on
2 limes and 1 tablespoon chopped
    fresh cilantro, to garnish

FOR THE SALSA VERDE
1 small onion, quartered
1 bunch fresh cilantro
1 teaspoon crushed garlic
1 tablespoon olive oil

ginger root

onion

olive oil

garlic

fresh cilantro

raw jumbo shrimp

white wine

COOK'S TIP
Fresh ginger freezes well wrapped in plastic wrap or a plastic freezer bag. Dry ginger is not an acceptable substitute for fresh.

NUTRITIONAL NOTES
PER PORTION:

ENERGY 90 Kcals
FAT 2.8 g **SATURATED FAT** 0.5 g
CHOLESTEROL 183 mg
FIBER 0.21 g

1 Combine the white wine, ginger and garlic in a medium bowl. Add the shrimp, turning to coat them in the marinade. Cover and chill for 4–6 hours.

2 Make the salsa. Chop the onion coarsely in a food processor. Add the cilantro and garlic and process until finely chopped. With the motor running, pour in the oil through the feeder tube of the processor. When the salsa is thick and creamy, scrape it into a serving bowl and set aside.

3 Cook the shrimp on a medium grill for 5–6 minutes, turning them once. Divide the shrimp among four plates. Cut the limes in half lengthwise, then into wedges. Press the long edge of each wedge into the chopped fresh cilantro. Place two wedges on each plate. Serve with the salsa verde.

Fish and Vegetable Kebabs

This can make an attractive main dish or an appetizer for eight. Serve it on a bed of flavored or plain rice, if desired.

NUTRITIONAL NOTES
PER PORTION:

ENERGY 123 Kcals
FAT 3.5 g **SATURATED FAT** 0.6 g
CHOLESTEROL 154 mg
FIBER 2.6 g

Serves 4

INGREDIENTS
10 ounces cod fillets, or any other firm, white fish fillets
3 tablespoons lemon juice
1 teaspoon grated fresh ginger root
2 fresh green chiles, very finely chopped
1 tablespoon very finely chopped fresh cilantro
1 tablespoon very finely chopped fresh mint
1 teaspoon ground coriander
1 teaspoon salt
1 red bell pepper
1 green bell pepper
½ medium cauliflower
8–10 button mushrooms
8 cherry tomatoes
1 tablespoon vegetable oil
1 lime, quartered

cod fillets
lemon juice
ginger root
green chiles
fresh mint
ground coriander
salt
fresh cilantro
green bell pepper
cauliflower
button mushrooms
red bell pepper
cherry tomatoes
vegetable oil
lime

1 Using a sharp knife, cut the fish fillets into large, evenly sized chunks (small ones would fall apart too easily and would disintegrate).

2 In a large mixing bowl, blend together the lemon juice, ginger, chopped green chiles, fresh cilantro, mint, ground coriander and salt. Add the fish chunks and let marinate in a cool place for about 30 minutes.

3 Cut the red and green bell peppers into large squares and divide the cauliflower into individual florets.

4 Arrange the red and green bell peppers, cauliflower florets, mushrooms and cherry tomatoes alternately with the pieces of fish on four skewers.

5 Baste the kebabs with the oil and any remaining marinade. Cook over a medium-hot grill for 7–10 minutes, or until the fish is cooked right through. Garnish with the lime quarters, and serve the kebabs either on their own or with rice.

Marinated Monkfish and Mussel Skewers

The marinade will make the monkfish both deliciously flavored and quicker to grill, so observe the cooking time closely.

Serves 4

INGREDIENTS
1 pound monkfish, skinned
   and boned
1 teaspoon olive oil
2 tablespoons lemon juice
1 teaspoon paprika
1 garlic clove, crushed
4 slices turkey bacon
8 cooked mussels
8 large raw shrimp
1 tablespoon chopped fresh dill
salt and freshly ground black pepper
lemon wedges, to garnish
salad and rice, to serve

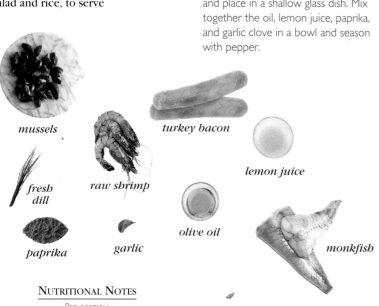

mussels

turkey bacon

fresh
dill

raw shrimp

lemon juice

olive oil

paprika

garlic

monkfish

NUTRITIONAL NOTES
PER PORTION:

ENERGY 164 Kcals
FAT 2.2 g SATURATED FAT 0.5 g
CHOLESTEROL 91 mg
FIBER 0

COOK'S TIP
If you thread your kebabs onto two parallel skewers they are easier to turn over.

1 Cut the monkfish into 1-inch cubes and place in a shallow glass dish. Mix together the oil, lemon juice, paprika, and garlic clove in a bowl and season with pepper.

2 Pour the marinade over the fish and toss to coat evenly. Cover and let sit in a cool place for 30 minutes.

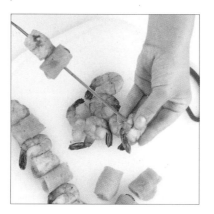

3 Cut the turkey bacon slices in half and wrap each strip around a mussel. Thread onto skewers alternating with the fish cubes and raw shrimp.

4 Cook the kebabs over a hot grill for 7–8 minutes, turning once and basting with the marinade. Sprinkle with chopped dill and salt. Garnish with the lemon wedges and serve with salad and rice.

Baked Potatoes with Spicy Cottage Cheese

Always choose a variety of potato recommended for baking—this recipe requires that the texture of the potato not be too dry.

NUTRITIONAL NOTES
PER PORTION:

ENERGY 311 Kcals
FAT 3.6 g **SATURATED FAT** 0.75 g
CHOLESTEROL 2.5 mg
FIBER 4.8 g

Serves 4

INGREDIENTS
4 medium baking potatoes
1 cup low-fat cottage cheese
2 teaspoons tomato paste
½ teaspoon ground cumin
½ teaspoon ground coriander
½ teaspoon chili powder
½ teaspoon salt
1 tablespoon corn oil
½ teaspoon mixed onion and
    mustard seeds
3 curry leaves
2 tablespoons water
mixed salad greens, fresh cilantro
    sprigs, lemon wedges and
    quartered tomatoes, to garnish

baking potatoes

low-fat cottage cheese

tomato paste

ground cumin

ground coriander

chili powder

curry leaves

corn oil

salt

1 Wash the potatoes, pat dry and make a slit in the middle of each one. Prick the potatoes a few times with a fork, then wrap them individually in foil. Cook over a medium-hot grill for about 1 hour, until soft.

2 Transfer the cottage cheese to a dish and set aside. In a separate bowl, combine the tomato paste, ground cumin, ground coriander, chili powder and salt.

3 Heat the corn oil in a small saucepan for 1 minute. Add the mixed onion and mustard seeds and the curry leaves, and make sure they are covered with the oil. When the leaves become dark, add the tomato paste mixture and lower the heat. Add the water and mix.

4 Cook for another minute, then pour the spicy tomato mixture onto the cottage cheese and blend everything together well.

5 Unwrap the cooked potatoes and divide the cottage cheese equally among them. Garnish with mixed salad greens, fresh cilantro sprigs, lemon wedges and tomato quarters.

VARIATION

Potatoes in their skins make a delicious vegetarian alternative to grilled meat and fish. They are naturally low in fat and are full of energy as they are very high in carbohydrates. They are also extremely versatile, and you can eat them with any topping.

Sweet-and-Sour Vegetables with Tofu

The marinade for these kebabs is a honey- and chili-seasoned oil that makes a delicious contrast with the vegetable and fruit selection. It creates a truly sweet and sour flavor.

Serves 4

INGREDIENTS
1 green bell pepper, cut into squares
1 yellow bell pepper, cut into squares
8 cherry, or 4 medium, tomatoes
8 cauliflower florets
8 fresh or canned pineapple chunks
8 cubes tofu
boiled rice, to serve (optional)

FOR THE MARINADE
1 tablespoon vegetable oil
2 tablespoons lemon juice
1 teaspoon salt
1 teaspoon freshly ground
    black pepper
1 tablespoon honey
2 tablespoons chili sauce

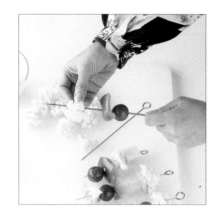

1 Thread the prepared vegetables, pineapple and tofu cubes onto four skewers, alternating the ingredients.

tofu

yellow bell pepper

cherry tomatoes

cauliflower

vegetable oil

lemon juice

pineapple

green bell pepper

salt

black pepper

honey

chile sauce

NUTRITIONAL NOTES
PER PORTION:

ENERGY 75 Kcals
FAT 2.6 g **SATURATED FAT** 0.4 g
CHOLESTEROL 0
FIBER 2.1 g

2 Prepare the marinade. Mix together all the ingredients. If the mixture is too thick, add 1 tablespoon water to dilute it a little.

3 Brush the skewers with the seasoned oil, ready for grilling. Cook on a hot grill for 10 minutes, until the vegetables begin to char slightly, turning the skewers often and basting with the seasoned oil. Serve on a bed of plain boiled rice, if you like.

Cassava and Vegetable Kebabs

This is an attractive and delicious assortment of African vegetables, marinated in a spicy garlic sauce. If cassava is unavailable, use sweet potato or yam. Serve with rice or couscous.

NUTRITIONAL NOTES
PER PORTION:

ENERGY 144 Kcals
FAT 3.3 g **SATURATED FAT** 0.5 g
CHOLESTEROL 0
FIBER 2.7 g

Serves 4

INGREDIENTS
6 ounces cassava
1 onion, cut into wedges
1 eggplant, cut into bite-size pieces
1 zucchini, sliced
1 ripe plantain, sliced
½ red bell pepper, sliced
½ green bell pepper, sliced
16 cherry tomatoes
rice or couscous, to serve

FOR THE MARINADE
4 tablespoons lemon juice
4 tablespoons olive oil
3–4 tablespoons soy sauce
1 tablespoon tomato paste
1 green chile, seeded and
    finely chopped
½ onion, grated
2 garlic cloves, crushed
1 teaspoon pumpkin pie spice
pinch of dried thyme

1 Peel the cassava and cut into bite-size pieces. Place in a bowl, cover with boiling water and let blanch for 5 minutes. Drain well. Place all the vegetables and the cassava, (but not the cherry tomatoes) in a large bowl and mix with your hands to distribute all the vegetables evenly.

cassava *eggplant* *zucchini* *plantain* *red bell pepper*

green bell pepper *cherry tomatoes* *lemon juice* *olive oil* *soy sauce*

tomato paste *garlic cloves* *onion* *green chile* *mixed spice* *dried thyme*

2 Blend together all the marinade ingredients and pour over the vegetables. Set aside for 1–2 hours.

3 Thread all the vegetables and cherry tomatoes onto eight skewers. Cook on a hot grill for 15 minutes, until tender, turning frequently and basting occasionally. Serve with rice or couscous.

Red Bean and Mushroom Burgers

Vegetarians and meat eaters alike will enjoy these healthy, low-fat veggie burgers. Served with salad, pita bread and plain yogurt, they make a substantial meal.

NUTRITIONAL NOTES
PER PORTION:

ENERGY 128 Kcals
FAT 3.4 g SATURATED FAT 0.5 g
CHOLESTEROL 0
FIBER 6.6 g

COOK'S TIP
These burgers are not quite as firm as meat burgers, and will need careful handling on the grill unless you use a wire rack.

Serves 4

INGREDIENTS

1 tablespoon olive oil, plus extra
    for brushing
1 small onion, finely chopped
1 garlic clove, crushed
1 teaspoon ground cumin
1 teaspoon ground coriander
1/2 teaspoon ground turmeric
1 1/2 cups finely chopped mushrooms
14-ounce can red kidney beans
2 tablespoons chopped
    fresh cilantro
whole-wheat flour
salt and freshly ground black pepper
low-fat plain yogurt, pita bread and
    salad, to serve

olive oil

onion

ground cumin

ground coriander

red kidney beans

ground turmeric

mushrooms

garlic

fresh cilantro

1 Heat the olive oil in a frying pan and sauté the chopped onion and garlic over moderate heat, stirring, until softened. Add the spices and cook for 1 minute more, stirring continuously.

2 Add the chopped mushrooms and cook, stirring, until softened and the mixture has become dry. Remove the pan from the heat and empty the contents into a large bowl.

3 Drain the beans thoroughly, place them in a bowl and mash with a fork.

4 Stir the kidney beans into the frying pan, with the chopped fresh cilantro, and mix thoroughly. Season the mixture well with plenty of salt and freshly ground black pepper.

5 Using floured hands, form the mixture into four flat burger shapes. If the mixture is too sticky to handle, mix in a little whole-wheat flour.

6 Lightly brush the burgers with olive oil and cook on a hot grill for 8–10 minutes, turning once, until golden brown. Serve with a spoonful of yogurt, pita bread and a green salad, if desired.

Herbed Polenta with Grilled Tomatoes

This recipe combines golden polenta with fresh summer herbs and sweet grilled tomatoes.

Serves 4

INGREDIENTS

3 cups vegetable stock or water
1 teaspoon salt
1 cup instant polenta
2 teaspoons butter
5 tablespoons mixed chopped fresh
    parsley, chives and basil, plus
    extra, to garnish
1 teaspoon olive oil
4 large plum or beef tomatoes, halved
salt and freshly ground black pepper

stock

salt

olive oil

plum tomatoes

polenta

butter

fresh basil

fresh parsley

fresh chives

NUTRITIONAL NOTES

PER PORTION:

ENERGY 185 Kcals
FAT 4.3 g **SATURATED FAT** 1.49 g
CHOLESTEROL 0
FIBER 0.5 g

1 Prepare the polenta in advance: place the water or stock in a pan, with the salt, and bring to a boil. Reduce the heat and stir in the polenta.

2 Stir constantly over moderate heat for 5 minutes, until the polenta begins to thicken and come away from the sides of the pan.

COOK'S TIP

Any mixture of fresh herbs can be used, or try using just basil or chives alone for a really distinctive flavor.

3 Remove from the heat and stir in the butter, herbs and black pepper.

4 Lightly grease a wide dish, add the polenta and spread out evenly. Once set, turn out and cut into shapes. Brush the tomatoes and polenta with oil and season. Cook on a medium-hot grill for 5 minutes, turning once. Serve garnished with fresh herbs.

Tofu Steaks

These tofu steaks are so full of Japanese flavor, they will please even the most committed meat eater. They cook quickly, too.

Serves 4

INGREDIENTS
1 package fresh tofu
    (4 x 3¾ x 1¼-inch), 11 ounces
    drained weight
2 scallions, thinly sliced,
    to garnish
mixed salad greens, to garnish

FOR THE MARINADE
3 tablespoons sake
2 tablespoons soy sauce
1 teaspoon sesame oil
1 garlic clove, crushed
1 tablespoon grated fresh ginger root
1 scallion, finely chopped

tofu   *scallions*

sake

soy sauce

sesame oil   *garlic*

ginger root

NUTRITIONAL NOTES
PER PORTION:

ENERGY 59 Kcals
FAT 3.6 g **SATURATED FAT** 0.4 g
CHOLESTEROL 0
FIBER 0

1 Wrap the tofu in a clean dish towel and place between two plates. Set aside for 30 minutes to remove any excess water.

2 Slice the tofu horizontally into 12 steaks. Set aside. Mix the ingredients for the marinade in a large bowl. Add the tofu to the bowl in a single layer and marinate for 30 minutes. Drain the tofu steaks and reserve the marinade to use for basting.

3 Cook the steaks on a hot grill for 3 minutes on each side, basting regularly with the marinade.

4 Arrange three tofu steaks on each plate. Any remaining marinade can be heated in a pan and then poured over the steaks. Sprinkle with the scallions and garnish with mixed salad greens. Serve immediately.

COOK'S TIP
Tofu is easily obtainable from supermarkets and health food stores, and is an ideal alternative to meat.

Summer Vegetables with Yogurt Pesto

Charbroiled vegetables make a meal on their own, or are delicious served as a Mediterranean-style accompaniment to grilled meats and fish.

COOK'S TIP

Baby vegetables make excellent candidates for grilling whole, so look for baby eggplant and bell peppers in particular. There's no need to salt the eggplant if they're small.

NUTRITIONAL NOTES

PER PORTION:

ENERGY 95 Kcals
FAT 3.5 g **SATURATED FAT** 0.9 g
CHOLESTEROL 3 mg
FIBER 3.4 g

Serves 4

INGREDIENTS
2 small eggplant
2 large zucchini
1 red bell pepper
1 yellow bell pepper
1 fennel bulb
1 red onion
2 teaspoons olive oil
salt and freshly ground black pepper

FOR THE YOGURT PESTO
2/3 cup fat-free plain yogurt
1 tablespoon pesto

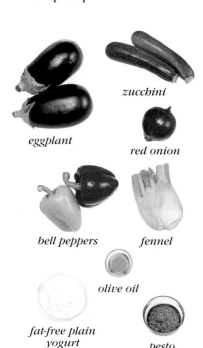

zucchini

eggplant

red onion

bell peppers   *fennel*

olive oil

fat-free plain yogurt

pesto

1 Cut the eggplant into ½-inch slices. Sprinkle with salt and let drain for about 30 minutes. Rinse well in cold running water and pat dry.

2 Use a sharp kitchen knife to cut the zucchini in half lengthwise. Cut the bell peppers in half, removing the seeds but leaving the stalks intact.

3 Slice the fennel bulb and the red onion into thick wedges, using a sharp kitchen knife.

4 Stir the yogurt and pesto lightly together in a serving bowl, to make a marbled sauce. Set aside.

5 Arrange the vegetables on the hot grill, brush with the olive oil and sprinkle with plenty of salt and freshly ground black pepper.

6 Cook the vegetables until golden brown and tender, turning occasionally. The eggplant and bell peppers will take 6–8 minutes to cook, and the zucchini, onion and fennel will take 4–5 minutes. Serve the vegetables immediately, with the yogurt pesto.

Vegetable Kebabs with Mustard and Honey

A colorful mixture of vegetables and tofu, skewered, glazed and grilled until tender.

NUTRITIONAL NOTES

PER PORTION:

ENERGY 202 Kcals
FAT 0.47 g **SATURATED FAT** 0.77 g
CHOLESTEROL 0
FIBER 1.4 g

Serves 4

INGREDIENTS
1 yellow bell pepper
2 small zucchini
8-ounce piece firm tofu
8 cherry tomatoes
8 button mushrooms
1 tablespoon whole-grain mustard
1 tablespoon honey
2 tablespoons olive oil
salt and freshly ground black pepper
lime segments and flat-leaf parsley,
    to garnish
rice, to serve (optional)

zucchini

*cherry
tomatoes*

honey

yellow bell pepper

tofu

olive oil

*whole-grain
mustard*

*button
mushrooms*

1 Cut the pepper in half and remove the seeds. Cut each half into eight pieces.

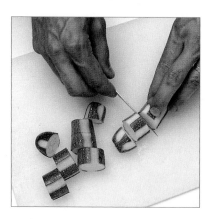

2 Trim the zucchini and peel them decoratively, if you like. Cut each zucchini into eight chunks.

3 Rinse the tofu under cold running water and drain well. Cut the tofu into neat, square pieces of a similar size to the vegetables.

4 Thread the bell pepper pieces, zucchini chunks, tofu, cherry tomatoes and mushrooms alternately onto four metal or wooden skewers.

5 Whisk the mustard, honey and olive oil in a small bowl. Add salt and pepper to taste.

6 Brush the kebabs with the mustard and honey glaze. Cook over a hot grill for eight minutes, turning once or twice during cooking. Serve with a mixture of long-grain and wild rice, and garnish with lime segments and parsley.

Summer Pasta Salad

Tender young vegetables with pasta in a light dressing make a delicious accompaniment to grilled chicken or fish.

Serves 4

INGREDIENTS
8 ounces fusilli or other dried
    pasta shapes
4 ounces baby carrots, trimmed
    and halved
4 ounces baby corn,
    halved lengthwise
2 ounces snow peas
4 ounces young asparagus
    spears, trimmed
4 scallions, trimmed
    and shredded
2 teaspoons white wine vinegar
2 teaspoons olive oil
1 tablespoon whole-grain mustard
salt and freshly ground black pepper

scallions

fusilli

young asparagus

whole-grain mustard

baby carrots

white wine vinegar

baby corn

olive oil

snow peas

1 Bring a large pan of salted water to a boil. Add the pasta and cook for 10–12 minutes, until just tender. Meanwhile, cook the carrots and corn in a second pan of boiling salted water for 5 minutes.

2 Add the snow peas and asparagus to the carrot mixture and cook for 2–3 minutes more. Drain all the vegetables and refresh under cold running water. Drain again.

3 Pour the vegetable mixture into a bowl, add the scallions and toss.

NUTRITIONAL NOTES

PER PORTION:

ENERGY 238 Kcals
FAT 3.2 g **SATURATED FAT** 0.4 g
CHOLESTEROL 0
FIBER 3.75 g

4 Drain the pasta, refresh it under cold running water and drain again. Toss with the vegetables. Mix the vinegar, olive oil and mustard in a jar. Add salt and pepper to taste, close the jar tightly and shake well. Pour the dressing over the salad. Toss well and serve.

Marinated Cucumber Salad

Sprinkling the cucumbers with salt draws out some of the water and makes them less bitter.

Serves 4

INGREDIENTS
2 medium cucumbers
1 tablespoon salt
½ cup granulated sugar
⅔ cup dry cider
1 tablespoon cider vinegar
3 tablespoons chopped fresh dill
pinch of pepper

dry cider

granulated sugar

fresh dill

cucumbers

cider vinegar

salt

1 Slice the cucumbers thinly and place them in a colander, sprinkling salt between each layer. Put the colander over a bowl and let drain for about 1 hour.

2 Thoroughly rinse the cucumber under cold running water to remove excess salt, then pat dry with absorbent paper towels.

NUTRITIONAL NOTES
PER PORTION:

ENERGY 41 Kcals
FAT 0.08 g **SATURATED FAT** 0
CHOLESTEROL 0
FIBER 0.4 g

COOK'S TIP

Try to eat this salad while it is as fresh as possible, as the vinegar will make the cucumber soft and discolored if left too long.

3 Gently heat the sugar, cider and vinegar in a saucepan until the sugar has dissolved. Remove from the heat and let cool. Put the cucumber slices in a bowl, pour the cider mixture over them and let marinate for 2 hours.

4 Drain the cucumber and sprinkle with the dill and pepper to taste. Mix well and transfer to a serving dish. Chill in the refrigerator until ready to serve.

Fruity Rice Salad

This appetizing and colorful rice salad, combining many different flavors, is ideal for a barbecue.

Serves 4

INGREDIENTS

1 cup mixed brown and wild rice
1 yellow bell pepper, seeded
  and diced
1 bunch scallions, chopped
3 celery stalks, chopped
1 large beefsteak tomato, chopped
2 Granny Smith apples, chopped
3/4 cup dried apricots, chopped
2/3 cup raisins
2 tablespoons unsweetened
  apple juice
2 tablespoons dry sherry
2 tablespoons light soy sauce
dash of Tabasco sauce
2 tablespoons chopped fresh parsley
1 tablespoon chopped fresh rosemary
salt and freshly ground black pepper

1 Cook the rice in a large saucepan of lightly salted boiling water for about 30 minutes (or according to the instructions on the package), until tender. Rinse the rice under cold running water to cool quickly, then drain thoroughly.

2 Place the pepper, scallions, celery, tomato, apples, apricots, raisins and the cooked rice in a serving bowl and mix well.

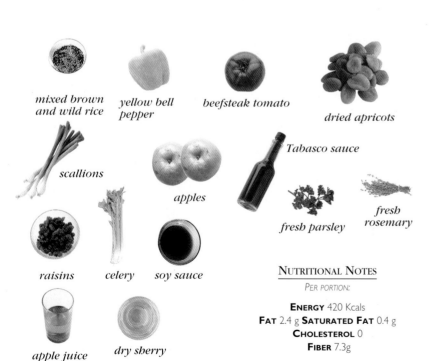

mixed brown and wild rice

yellow bell pepper

beefsteak tomato

dried apricots

scallions

apples

Tabasco sauce

fresh parsley

fresh rosemary

raisins

celery

soy sauce

apple juice

dry sherry

<u>NUTRITIONAL NOTES</u>

PER PORTION:

ENERGY 420 Kcals
FAT 2.4 g **SATURATED FAT** 0.4 g
CHOLESTEROL 0
FIBER 7.3g

3 Now make the dressing. In a small bowl, mix together the apple juice, dry sherry, soy sauce, Tabasco sauce, chopped fresh parsley, chopped fresh rosemary, salt and freshly ground black pepper.

4 Pour the salad dressing over the prepared rice, vegetable and fruit mixture. Toss all the ingredients together gently but thoroughly. Serve immediately, or cover and chill in the refrigerator for 1–2 hours before serving.

Bulgur and Mint Salad

Also known as cracked wheat, burghul or pourgouri, bulgur has already been partially cooked, so it requires only a short period of soaking before serving.

Serves 4

INGREDIENTS

1²/₃ cups bulgur
4 tomatoes, chopped
4 small zucchini, thinly
    sliced lengthwise
4 scallions, sliced on the diagonal
8 dried apricots, chopped
¹/₄ cup raisins
juice of 1 lemon
2 tablespoons tomato juice
3 tablespoons chopped fresh mint
1 garlic clove, crushed
salt and freshly ground black pepper
sprig of fresh mint, to garnish

dried apricots   *raisins*

lemon juice   *zucchini*   *scallions*   *tomatoes*

tomato juice   *fresh mint*   *bulgur*   *garlic*

COOK'S TIP

Bulgur is made from whole-wheat grain, including the wheat germ, and is a rich source of nutrients. It has a distinctive flavor and can be used in a variety of dishes.

NUTRITIONAL NOTES
PER PORTION:
ENERGY 227 Kcals
FAT 1.27 g **SATURATED FAT** 0.1 g
CHOLESTEROL 0
FIBER 2.9 g

1 Put the bulgur into a large bowl. Add enough cold water to come 1 inch above the surface of the wheat. Let soak for 30 minutes, then drain well and squeeze out any excess water in a clean dish towel.

2 Meanwhile, plunge the tomatoes into boiling water and leave for 1 minute, then plunge into cold water. Remove the skins, which should now slip off easily. Halve the tomatoes, remove the seeds and cores, and roughly chop the flesh.

3 Now add the tomatoes, zucchini, scallions, apricots and raisins to the soaked and drained bulgur. Stir well but gently, until the ingredients are thoroughly combined.

4 Put the lemon and tomato juice, mint, garlic and seasoning into a small bowl and whisk together with a fork. Pour over the salad and mix well. Chill in the refrigerator for at least 1 hour. Serve garnished with a sprig of mint.

Watercress and Potato Salad

New potatoes are equally good hot or cold, and this colorful, nutritious salad is an ideal way to make the most of them. Everyone loves a potato salad with their barbecue.

Serves 4

INGREDIENTS
1 pound small new
   potatoes, unpeeled
1 bunch watercress
8 ounces cherry tomatoes, halved
2 tablespoons pumpkin seeds
3 tablespoons fat-free fromage frais
1 tablespoon cider vinegar
1 teaspoon brown sugar
salt and paprika

new potatoes

watercress

brown sugar

pumpkin seeds

cherry tomatoes

fat-free fromage frais

cider vinegar

NUTRITIONAL NOTES
PER PORTION:

ENERGY 146 Kcals
FAT 4.4 g **SATURATED FAT** 0.8 g
CHOLESTEROL 0
FIBER 3.2 g

1 Cook the new potatoes over low heat in lightly salted boiling water for 20–30 minutes, depending on their size, until just tender. Then drain them and let cool.

COOK'S TIP
New potatoes are delicious cooked and eaten with their skins still on. Some people, however, don't like the skins, in which case you should cook them with the skins on and then peel them when they have cooled. Serve this salad at room temperature.

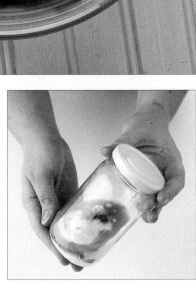

2 Toss together the potatoes, watercress, tomatoes and pumpkin seeds in a mixing bowl.

3 Place the fromage frais, vinegar, sugar, salt and paprika in a screw-top jar and shake well to mix. Pour over the salad just before serving.

Fennel and Herb Coleslaw

The addition of fennel to this coleslaw gives it a distinctive anise flavor that pairs well with grilled meat. There is no mayonnaise in this salad, but it is just as flavorful without—as well as being much lighter and healthier.

Serves 4

INGREDIENTS
1 fennel bulb
2 scallions
½ white cabbage
2 celery stalks
3 carrots
½ cup golden raisins
½ teaspoon caraway
    seeds (optional)
1 tablespoon chopped fresh parsley
1 tablespoon olive oil
1 teaspoon lemon juice
shreds of scallion, to garnish

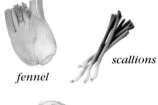
fennel

scallions

white cabbage

golden raisins

lemon juice

celery

carrots

fresh parsley

olive oil

COOK'S TIP
The best olive oil that you can use is extra virgin olive oil.

1 Using a really sharp knife, cut the fennel bulbs into thin slices. Then slice the scallions finely. Put to one side for use later.

NUTRITIONAL NOTES
PER PORTION:

ENERGY 94 Kcals
FAT 3.2 g **SATURATED FAT** 0.4 g
CHOLESTEROL 0
FIBER 3.7 g

2 Slice the cabbage and celery finely and cut the carrots into julienne strips. Place in a serving bowl together with the other vegetables.

3 Add the golden raisins and caraway seeds, if using. Stir in the chopped parsley, olive oil and lemon juice and mix well. Cover and chill for 3 hours to allow the flavors to mingle. Serve, garnished with the scallion shreds.

Mango, Tomato and Red Onion Salad

The underripe mango has a subtle sweetness that blends well with the tomato.

Serves 4

INGREDIENTS
1 firm underripe mango
2 large tomatoes or 1 beefsteak
    tomato, sliced
$\frac{1}{2}$ red onion, sliced into rings
$\frac{1}{2}$ cucumber, peeled and thinly sliced
1 tablespoon sunflower or
    vegetable oil
1 tablespoon lemon juice
1 garlic clove, crushed
$\frac{1}{2}$ teaspoon hot pepper sauce
sugar, to taste
salt and freshly ground black pepper
snipped chives, to garnish

mango

tomatoes

red onion

cucumber

garlic

hot pepper sauce

oil

lemon juice

sugar

1 Cut away two thick slices from either side of the mango stone and cut into smaller slices. Peel the skin from the slices. Arrange the mango, tomato, onion and cucumber slices in a decorative design on a serving plate.

VARIATION

Slices of avocado would make a delicious alternative to the mango. However, avocados have a very high fat content, so don't try this if you are on a low-fat diet!

NUTRITIONAL NOTES

PER PORTION:

ENERGY 57 Kcals
FAT 2.9 g **SATURATED FAT** 0.3 g
CHOLESTEROL 0
FIBER 1.6 g

2 Blend the oil, lemon juice, garlic, hot pepper sauce, salt and black pepper in a blender or food processor, or place in a small jar and shake vigorously. Add a pinch of sugar to taste and mix again.

3 Pour the dressing over the salad and garnish with the snipped chives.

Fattoush

This simple peasant salad is a popular dish all over Syria and the Lebanon. It will complement the flavors of any barbecue party.

Serves 4

INGREDIENTS
1 yellow or red bell pepper
1 large cucumber
4–5 tomatoes
1 bunch scallions
2 tablespoons finely chopped
    fresh parsley
2 tablespoons finely chopped
    fresh mint
2 tablespoons finely chopped
    fresh cilantro
2 garlic cloves, crushed
1 tablespoon olive oil
juice of 2 lemons
salt and freshly ground black pepper
2 pita breads, to serve

1 Halve and core the bell pepper, discarding the seeds, and slice it thinly. Coarsely chop the cucumber and tomatoes. Place the pepper, cucumber and tomatoes in a large salad bowl.

pepper

cucumber

fresh parsley

fresh cilantro

tomatoes

scallions

lemon juice

olive oil

garlic

fresh mint

2 Trim and slice the scallions. Add to the bell pepper, cucumber and tomatoes with the finely chopped parsley, mint and cilantro.

3 To make the dressing, blend the garlic with the olive oil and lemon juice, then season to taste with salt and black pepper.

VARIATION

After toasting the pita bread until crisp, crush it in your hand and sprinkle it on the salad before serving, for a more traditional touch.

NUTRITIONAL NOTES
PER PORTION:
ENERGY 164 Kcals
FAT 3.8 g **SATURATED FAT** 0.5 g
CHOLESTEROL 0
FIBER 4.3 g

COOK'S TIP

If you have plenty of herbs on hand, you can add as many as you like to this aromatic salad.

4 Pour the dressing over the salad and toss lightly to mix. Toast the pita bread on the grill until crisp and serve it with the salad.

DESSERTS

Pineapple Wedges with Allspice and Lime

Fresh pineapple is easy to prepare and always looks very attractive, so this dish is perfect for easy outdoor entertaining.

Serves 4

INGREDIENTS
1 medium-size ripe pineapple
1 lime
1 tablespoon dark brown sugar
1 teaspoon ground allspice

ground allspice

pineapple

dark brown sugar

lime

1 Cut the pineapple lengthwise into quarters and remove the core.

2 Slice the flesh away from the skin. Cut into slices and arrange decoratively upon the skin.

VARIATION
For a hot dish, place the pineapple slices on a wire rack, sprinkle them with the lime juice, sugar and allspice, and place them on a hot grill for 3-4 minutes, until golden and bubbling. Sprinkle with shreds of lime zest and serve.

NUTRITIONAL NOTES
PER PORTION:

ENERGY 55 Kcals
FAT 0.2 g SATURATED FAT 0
CHOLESTEROL 0
FIBER 1.1 g

3 Remove a few shreds of rind from the lime and then squeeze out the juice.

4 Sprinkle the pineapple with the lime juice and rind, sugar and allspice. Serve immediately, or chill for up to an hour.

Baked Bananas with Spicy Vanilla Butter

Baked bananas are a must for the grill—they're so easy because they bake in their own skins and need no preparation at all. A flavored butter melting over them adds richness, or you can use jam or honey.

Serves 4

INGREDIENTS
4 bananas
6 green cardamom pods
1 vanilla bean
finely grated zest of 1 small orange
2 tablespoons brandy or orange juice
4 tablespoons light brown sugar
4 teaspoons butter
crème fraîche or low-fat plain yogurt,
    to serve

brandy

butter

orange

*green cardamom
pods*

bananas

vanilla pod

*light brown
sugar*

NUTRITIONAL NOTES
PER PORTION:

ENERGY 177 Kcals
FAT 4.4 g **SATURATED FAT** 2.9 g
CHOLESTEROL 10.1 mg
FIBER 0.9 g

1 Place the bananas, in their skins, on the hot grill and leave for about 6–8 minutes, turning occasionally, until they are turning brownish-black.

2 Meanwhile, split the cardamom pods and remove the seeds. Crush lightly in a mortar and pestle.

3 Split the vanilla bean lengthwise and scrape out the tiny seeds. Mix with the cardamom seeds, orange zest, brandy or juice, sugar and butter, into a thick paste.

4 Slit the skin of each banana, open out slightly and spoon in a little of the paste. Serve with a spoonful of crème fraîche or plain yogurt.

Baked Apples in Honey and Lemon

Tender baked apples with a classic flavoring of lemon and honey make a simple dessert for cooking on the grill. Serve with custard or a spoonful of low-fat yogurt, if desired.

Serves 4

INGREDIENTS
4 medium cooking apples
1 tablespoon honey
grated zest and juice of 1 lemon
1 tablespoon butter, melted

lemon

cooking apples

butter

honey

NUTRITIONAL NOTES

PER PORTION:

ENERGY 137 Kcals
FAT 3.3 g **SATURATED FAT** 2.1 g
CHOLESTEROL 8.8 mg
FIBER 4.4 g

1 Remove the cores from the apples, leaving them whole. Cut four squares of double-thickness baking foil, to wrap the apples. Brush the foil with butter.

2 Using a channel knife or sharp knife, cut vertical lines through the surface of the apple skin at regular intervals.

3 Combine the honey, lemon zest, juice and butter in a small bowl.

4 Spoon the mixture into the apples and wrap in foil, sealing the edges securely. Cook on a hot grill for 20 minutes, until the apples are tender.

Frudités with Honey Dip

A luscious dessert consisting of a selection of fresh summer fruits, this is simply delicious. It makes an equally delicious breakfast.

Serves 4

INGREDIENTS
1 cup low-fat plain yogurt
3 tablespoons honey
selection of fresh fruit for dipping
   such as apples, tangerines, grapes,
   figs, pears and strawberries

low-fat plain yogurt

honey

apples

pears

grapes

tangerines

strawberries

figs

1 Place the yogurt in a dish, beat until smooth, then stir in the honey, leaving a little marbled effect.

2 Prepare the fruit pieces. Peel the tangerines and divide the segments. Cut the pears in half, remove the seeds and halve again.

NUTRITIONAL NOTES

PER PORTION OF DIP:

ENERGY 67.5 Kcals
FAT 0.5 g **SATURATED FAT** 0.3 g
CHOLESTEROL 2.5 mg
FIBER 0

3 Cut the rest of the fruits into wedges or bite-size pieces, or leave some whole.

4 Arrange the fresh fruit on a platter with the bowl of honey dip in the center. Serve chilled.

Papaya Skewers with a Passion Fruit Coulis

Tropical fruits, full of natural sweetness, make a simple, exotic dessert.

Serves 6

INGREDIENTS
3 ripe papayas
10 passion fruit or kiwi
2 tablespoons lime juice
2 tablespoons confectioners' sugar
2 tablespoons white rum
lime slices, to garnish

confectioners' sugar

white rum

papayas

passion fruit

lime

COOK'S TIP

If you are short of time, the passion fruit flesh can be used as it is, without puréeing or sieving. Simply scoop the flesh from the skins and mix it with the lime, sugar and rum. The kiwi will still need to be puréed, however.

1 Cut the papayas in half and scoop out the seeds. Peel them and cut the flesh into evenly sized chunks. Thread the chunks onto six skewers.

2 Halve eight of the passion fruit or kiwi and scoop out the flesh. Purée the flesh for a few seconds in a blender or food processor.

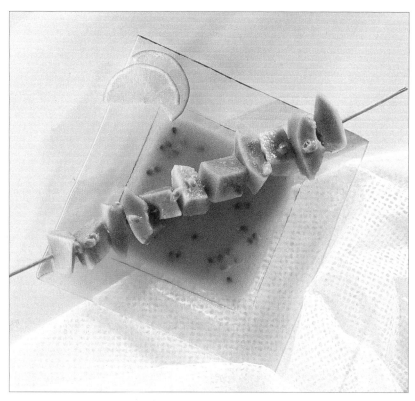

3 Press the pulp through a sieve and discard the seeds. Add the lime juice, confectioners' sugar and rum, then stir.

NUTRITIONAL NOTES

PER PORTION:

ENERGY 151 Kcals
FAT 0.8 g **SATURATED FAT** 0
CHOLESTEROL 0
FIBER 4.9 g

4 When the sugar has dissolved in the mixture, spoon a little coulis onto six serving plates. Place the skewers on top. Scoop the flesh from the remaining passion fruit or kiwi and spoon it on top. Garnish with lime slices, and serve.

Passion Fruit and Raspberry Swirls

If passion fruit is not available, this simple dessert can be made with raspberries alone. It is absolutely delicious served chilled on a warm day.

Serves 4

INGREDIENTS
2¼ cups raspberries
2 passion fruit
1⅔ cups fat-free fromage frais
2 tablespoons sugar
4 raspberries and sprigs of mint,
   to decorate

raspberries   *passion fruit*

fat-free fromage frais   *sugar*

1 Mash the raspberries in a small bowl until the juice runs.

2 Scoop out the passion fruit pulp into a separate bowl with the fromage frais and sugar and mix well.

3 Spoon alternate spoonfuls of the raspberry pulp and the fromage frais mixture into stemmed glasses or one large serving dish.

4 Stir the pulp lightly to create a swirled effect. Decorate each dessert with a whole raspberry and a sprig of mint. Set in the refrigerator until ready to serve.

NUTRITIONAL NOTES
PER PORTION:

ENERGY 97 Kcals
FAT 0.6 g **SATURATED FAT** 0.2 g
CHOLESTEROL 1 mg
FIBER 3.9 g

COOK'S TIP
Overripe, slightly soft fruit can also be used in this recipe. Use frozen raspberries when fresh ones are not available, but thaw them first.

Fruit Crush with Fruit Kebabs

Fruit crush is just the answer on a sultry summer day, served with mouthwatering fruit kebabs.

NUTRITIONAL NOTES

Per portion:

ENERGY 216 Kcals
FAT 0.4 g **SATURATED FAT** 0.03 g
CHOLESTEROL 0
FIBER 1.2 g

Serves 6

INGREDIENTS
FOR THE FRUIT CRUSH
1¼ cups orange juice
1¼ cups pineapple juice
1¼ cups tropical fruit juice
2 cups lemonade
fresh pineapple slices and fresh
    cherries, to decorate

FOR THE FRUIT KEBABS
24 small strawberries
24 green seedless grapes
12 marshmallows
1 kiwi, peeled and cut into
    12 wedges
1 banana
1 tablespoon lemon juice

1 To make the fruit crush, pour the orange juice and the pineapple juice into ice-cube trays and freeze them until they have become solid.

2 Combine the tropical fruit juice and lemonade in a large bowl. Put a mixture of the ice cubes in each glass, pour in the fruit crush and decorate each glass with the pineapple slices and the cherries.

3 To make the fruit kebabs, thread two strawberries, two grapes, a marshmallow and a wedge of kiwi onto each of 12 wooden skewers.

4 Peel the banana and cut it into 12 slices. Toss it in the lemon juice and thread onto the skewers. Serve them immediately with the fruit crush.

pineapple juice

kiwi fruit

lemon juice

banana

tropical fruit juice

lemonade

green grapes

orange juice

marshmallows

strawberries

Watermelon Sorbet

A slice of this colorful, tangy and refreshing sorbet is the perfect way to quench your thirst and cool down on a hot, sunny day.

Serves 4-6

INGREDIENTS
$\frac{1}{2}$ small watermelon, weighing about 2$\frac{1}{4}$ pounds
$\frac{1}{2}$ cup sugar
4 tablespoons cranberry juice or water
2 tablespoons lemon juice
sprigs of fresh mint, to decorate

cranberry juice

sugar

watermelon

lemon juice

1 Cut the watermelon into four to six equal-size wedges (depending on the number of servings you require). Scoop out the pink flesh, discarding the seeds but reserving the shell.

2 Line a freezer-proof bowl, about the same size as the melon, with plastic wrap. Arrange the melon skins in the bowl to re-form the shell, fitting them together snugly so that there are no gaps. Put in the freezer.

3 Put the sugar and cranberry juice or water in a saucepan and stir over low heat until the sugar dissolves. Bring to a boil and simmer for 5 minutes. Let the sugar syrup cool.

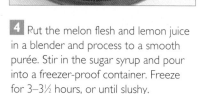

4 Put the melon flesh and lemon juice in a blender and process to a smooth purée. Stir in the sugar syrup and pour into a freezer-proof container. Freeze for 3–3$\frac{1}{2}$ hours, or until slushy.

5 Transfer the sorbet into a chilled bowl and whisk to break up the ice crystals. Return to the freezer for another 30 minutes, whisk again, then transfer to the melon shell and freeze until solid.

6 Remove from the freezer and let defrost at room temperature for 15 minutes. Take the melon out of the bowl and cut into wedges with a sharp, warmed knife. Decorate with sprigs of fresh mint and serve.

NUTRITIONAL NOTES
PER PORTION:

ENERGY 118 Kcals
FAT 0.5 g SATURATED FAT 0
CHOLESTEROL 0
FIBER 0.25 g

INDEX